THE PATCHWORK COMPANION

Master Key Skills with 14 Quilt Projects

Sandy Saengsuk

stashBOOKS
an imprint of C&T Publishing

Text, artwork, and instructional photography copyright © 2026 by Sandy Saengsuk

Lifestyle photography copyright © 2026 by C&T Publishing, Inc.

Publisher: Amy Barrett-Daffin

Creative Director: Gailen Runge

Senior Editor: Roxane Cerda

Editor: Madison Moore

Technical Editor: Debbie Rodgers

Cover/Book Designer: April Mostek

Production Coordinator: Zinnia Heinzmann

Illustrators: Kirstie Pettersen, and Sandy Saengsuk

Photography Coordinator: Rachel Ackley

Front cover photography by Lydia Nicholson

Lifestyle photography by Lydia Nicholson, unless otherwise noted

Lifestyle photography on pages 2 (top), 55, 62, and 77 (bottom) by Sandy Saengsuk

Instructional photography by Sandy Saengsuk, unless otherwise noted

Published by Stash Books, an imprint of C&T Publishing, Inc., P.O. Box 1456, Lafayette, CA 94549

Library of Congress Control Number: 2025049819

Library of Congress Cataloging-in-Publication Data is available upon request.

Printed in China

10 9 8 7 6 5 4 3 2 1

Dedication

To my husband, David, the best quilt-holder I could ever ask for.
Thank you for never saying no, even when it means standing at the edge of a cliff to capture the perfect quilt photo.

To my beautiful daughters, Helena and Anneliesia, who always believe their mommy can make anything beautiful. Your love and faith in me mean the world.

ACKNOWLEDGMENTS

A special thanks to C&T Publishing and Madison Moore, my editor, for being so patient and supportive throughout this journey. My deepest gratitude to Riley Blake Designs for their generosity in providing the beautiful fabrics for all the projects in this book. A special thanks to Kelly Morris, VP of Marketing at Riley Blake, and everyone in the RBD Design Room for always being willing to help with countless fabric requests and never once complaining. And of course, thank you to Aurifil thread for providing such gorgeous, high-quality thread that made the quilting in this book truly shine.

I'd also like to thank my family for their unwavering support through the entire book-writing process. It's been a labor of love, and not just from me, but from everyone in my family who has helped me get through it. I especially want to thank my dad, who is watching us from heaven, for always pushing us to be better because he truly believed there was nothing his daughters couldn't do. I imagine you're laughing at me writing a quilting book right now, all while enjoying your favorite chocolate cake and espresso.

A heartfelt thank you to my quilty friends, especially Christina Lee, for helping me push through my doubts. You are truly the best! I wouldn't be here without the quilting community and the endless inspiration shared with me. To the designers who unknowingly inspired me, just to name a few, SuzyQuilts, Brittany Lloyd, Sharon Holland, and so many more, thank you for lighting the way. A special shout out to the OG group and all of my quilty friends who supported me through the book writing process, you know who you are! And to Wendy Chow and Amanda Carye, thank you for getting me out of my shell and having me on your Quilt Buzz Podcast. That was honestly one of the scariest things I've ever done, but so much fun!

And finally, to all the magazine and Lookbook editors I've worked with, who have shaped me into who I am today: Marcela Loayza and the AGF Lookbook Team at Art Gallery Fabrics, who published my very first pattern, *Ixora Quilt*, back in early 2021, and so many more after those, Lorna Slessor at Love Patchwork & Quilting, Maddie Butler and RBD Influencer Team at Riley Blake Designs. Thank you all for your incredible support and belief in my work.

And thank you from the bottom of my heart for bringing this book into your life. I truly hope it inspires you to design, create, and make something beautiful that can inspire others. Your support means the world to me, and I am incredibly grateful that you've chosen to be part of this journey with me. I hope you enjoy every project and find joy in the process of bringing them to life. Thank you for making this dream a reality and for being a part of this wonderful quilting community.

Contents

QUILT PROJECTS

Introduction

Quilting has been a journey of discovery and joy for me: a passion that took root in an unexpected way and blossomed into a lifelong love. I'm thrilled to share that love with you through this book, where I've poured my heart and soul into each pattern and tip.

My quilting story began with the life-changing event of meeting my husband, and then moving to the coldest place I could find—Minnesota. The warm climate of my childhood town just outside Bangkok made quilts more of a novelty than a necessity, so quilting was never part of the plan. Fast forward to 2020: my mom moved to Minnesota to stay with us, and my mother-in-law was looking for a way to connect with her. With a language barrier between them, the options were quite limited until they finally decided on quilting. They started a project together, and I found myself jumping into help with just one quilt. But I soon discovered that quilting, much like life, is full of endless questions, challenges, and delightful surprises. One quilt turned into two, then three, and before I knew it, I was head over heels in love with the art of quilting. There's something magical about watching different colors and prints come together, forming a design that looks and feels right. It's a bit like painting with fabric.

My grandma never told me outright to embrace boldness, but she showed me through her favorite outfits. Whenever we went to the temple for special occasions, she would wear vibrant colors and striking patterns that radiated happiness. Her fearless approach to color has been a guiding light for me, inspiring many of the designs in this book. Quilting is the perfect outlet for my passion for bold, fearless colors and prints. Every quilt I make is an opportunity to experiment, mix and match, and discover new ways to express myself. I encourage you to embrace your creative instincts and let your personality shine through your fabric choices.

Whether you're a seasoned quilter or just starting your journey, you'll find a place here. As a visual learner, I know how important clear instructions and diagrams are for guiding you through each step. Each pattern focuses on specific skills, building your knowledge and confidence as you progress. By practicing the techniques covered in this book, you'll gain the foundational knowledge and skills needed to tackle almost any quilt.

Believe it or not, my non-English-speaking mom was my very first pattern tester. She not only completed the quilt with confidence but rarely needed to ask questions. That experience affirmed to me that with clear guidance, anyone can create something beautiful. Quilting is about creating something meaningful with your own two hands. This book is a celebration of that process, offering patterns and techniques that I've come to love and trust. I hope this book inspires you to try new techniques, embrace bold choices, and, most importantly, find joy in every stitch. Thank you for letting me be part of your quilting journey!

TOOLS *and* MATERIALS

SEWING MACHINE

My sewing machine is a little Janome named *Jenny*. Jenny has been with me through countless projects from the very beginning, and she still runs just fine. You don't need a fancy machine to make a quilt. As long as your machine can sew with an accurate ¼″ seam allowance, you're good to go. If you're looking to buy a new machine, you want the biggest throat space you can afford, especially if you're planning to quilt your own quilts. This gives you more flexibility to maneuver all the layers of a quilt through the machine.

QUILTING RULERS

When it comes to quilting, having the right rulers can make a big difference in cutting accuracy. A 6½˝ × 24˝ ruler is perfect for cutting the width of fabric (WOF) of quilting cotton (usually 42˝–44˝) and is often used to square up the quilt. A 6½˝ × 6½˝ ruler is great for sub-cutting smaller pieces and trimming blocks. Finally, a 12½˝ × 12½˝ ruler is just the right size for squaring up quilt blocks. With these basic sizes, you can tackle most cutting needs. As you develop as a quilter, you might find yourself favoring certain sizes more than others or even considering investing in specialty rulers. Ultimately, it all comes down to personal preference.

CUTTING TOOLS

Cutting Mat A self-healing cutting mat is a must-have for any quilter. It provides a safe surface for cutting fabric, protecting both your work surface and your rotary cutter blade. I recommend getting one that's at least 21˝ in length to comfortably accommodate the standard width of fabric (WOF). A 24˝ × 36˝ mat is a great size for most quilting projects.

Rotary Cutter Rotary cutters are the best choice for fast, efficient, and accurate cutting. I recommend a 45mm rotary cutter for most cutting and a small 28mm cutter for cutting curves.

Rotary Cutting Blades Get a cutting blade that matches your rotary cutter. A sharp blade makes a world of difference for clean, easy cuts and a smoother quilting experience. If you start to notice that the blade is dragging or dull, it's probably time for a change. A newer blade also helps protect your wrist, as it requires less effort to cut.

Fabric Scissors Scissors are great for snipping threads, as well as trimming small fabric edges or making precise cuts in delicate areas. Make sure to only use them for textiles!

NEEDLES AND THREADS

I suggest using 50wt thread with your sewing machine. A universal 80/12 or 90/14 needle will work great with this thread weight and most quilting fabrics.

Some quilters like to quilt or bind stitching by hand with big visible stitching and/or contrast thread, creating a bold and modern look. To achieve this, use a heavier cotton or wool thread, like 12wt or 8wt. When it comes to needles, choose ones like Gold Eye embroidery needles or Sashiko needles, which have larger eyes to handle thicker thread.

GENERAL TOOLS

Iron and Pressing Mat A wool pressing mat is a game-changer for well-pressed quilt blocks. The mat holds heat exceptionally well, so it reflects heat to both sides of the fabric. This makes pressing faster and helps set those seams perfectly. Any kind of iron will work—use what feels comfortable.

Hera Marker Hera markers are wooden or plastic tools that crease or indent fabric without leaving a residue, which means there's no need to worry about washing the marks away!

Fabric Markers There are lots of options for fabric markers: water-erasable, air-erasable, heat-erasable, you name it! Pick the one that best suits your project and fabric. Always test on a small fabric scrap first to ensure the marks disappear as expected.

Walking Foot A walking foot is an optional attachment that helps feed multiple layers of fabric evenly through the sewing machine. It's perfect for quilting or working with thick fabrics, preventing shifting and puckering for smooth, even stitches. If you're quilting with a domestic machine, investing in a walking foot is a great idea.

Pins Pins are essential tools for keeping everything aligned, preventing shifting, and ensuring your seams are accurate. Remove them as you sew to avoid any issues with your sewing machine.

Seam Ripper What kind of quilter would I be if I didn't mention a quilter's best friend, the seam ripper? It is a handy tool used to carefully remove stitches when you need to correct a mistake or take apart seams.

¼″ Foot A quarter-inch foot helps sew a precise ¼″ seam, the standard seam allowance in quilting. It often includes a guide to keep fabric edges aligned, making it easier to piece blocks accurately and ensure they fit together as intended.

FABRIC

Quilting cotton is used almost universally for quilts, and for good reason! It's durable, easy to work with, and comes in a wide variety of prints and colors. Cotton fabric also breathes well, making quilts soft and comfortable. It holds up beautifully over time, which is essential for a quilt that will be washed and loved.

More and more quilters are turning to other types of woven fabrics for their unique textures and slightly different appearance. These fabrics can bring fresh dimension to your projects and are a great way to explore new techniques, making each quilt a reflection of your personal style. Other woven fabrics have a looser weave and a softer, more textured feel compared to traditional quilting cotton, which is tightly woven and crisp. While quilting cotton is stable and easy to piece, other wovens can fray more easily and may shift during sewing. With a little starch and careful handling, though, they bring a cozy, handmade look and add beautiful texture to any quilt.

Please keep in mind that some of the exact fabrics shown in the quilt samples may no longer be available. If that happens, see it as an opportunity to put your own spin on the design. Choose colors and prints that speak to you, and let your fabric choices tell your story. That's what makes each quilt truly one of a kind.

BATTING

Batting, like everything else we talk about, really comes down to personal preference:

- If you want a weighted quilt, choose wool batting for its warmth and loft.
- If you want a breathable quilt for a warmer climate, 100% cotton batting is your best bet.
- If you want durability and texture, go for 80/20 cotton batting, as it combines the softness of cotton with the strength of polyester.
- If you're looking for an eco-friendly, silky soft feel with great breathability, bamboo batting might be your perfect choice. It is naturally hypoallergenic.

MISCELLANEOUS SEWING TOOLS

Here are a few of my favorite tools that aren't essential but can make the quilting process much faster and easier:

Thread Cutter A thread cutter works wonders when you're chain piecing. It's a quick and easy way to snip threads between pieces without having to stop and use scissors.

Rotating Cutting Mat A small cutting mat on a turntable base that spins makes it easy to trim blocks, especially half-square triangles, without having to lift or shift the fabric. It saves time, improves accuracy, and keeps the rotary cutter at a safe angle. It's also great for small spaces since there's no need to move around the table to get the right cutting angle.

Magnetic Cutting Mat A magnetic cutting mat provides an extra hold on your fabric and ruler, making it easier on your wrist while cutting. This feature is especially helpful when cutting curves or working on a large bed-sized quilt, where precision and comfort are key.

Specialty Rulers Having the perfectly right ruler for your projects is super convenient. I work with a lot of half-square triangles (HSTs) and strips, so I invested in a Slotted Trimmer and a Stripology ruler. They make cutting and trimming so much faster.

Seam Roller A seam roller is a handy tool that temporarily presses your seams, allowing you to sew your block together without making extra trips to the ironing station.

Smoothing Spray Flatter Smoothing Spray by Soak is a great product for keeping seams flat, especially when working with tiny pieces, curves, or lots of seams. It relaxes fabric fibers, helping your seams lie smooth without extra pressing.

Color Cards If you're using lots of solid fabrics, having a set of color cards will ensure you're buying the right fabric every time. They're incredibly helpful if you usually shop online since it can be hard to get an accurate sense of the color through a screen.

C120-Scuba
8 89333 12822 9
C120-HONEY
8 89333 05951 6
C120-Cinnamon
8 89333 02862 8
C120-BleachedDenim
8 89333 02815 4

Quilting BASICS

TERMS AND DEFINITIONS

Right Sides Together (RST) Aligning fabric so the *right* or exterior-facing sides of the fabric are put together. When you're using solid-colored quilting cotton, the right and wrong sides generally look the same.

Wrong Sides Together (WST) Aligning fabric so the wrong or interior-facing sides of the fabric are put together.

Piecing The term quilters use for sewing fabric pieces together, often forming blocks or patterns. Piecing is always done by putting two pieces of fabric right sides together, then sewing.

Quilt Top The term for the pieced front of a quilt before it is assembled into a finished quilt with batting and backing.

Backing The piece of (or pieced) fabric used for the back of a quilt.

Basting The term for temporarily securing layers of fabric together with stitches, spray, or safety pins. When basting a quilt sandwich (below), most quilters use basting spray or pins.

Quilt Sandwich The three layers of a finished quilt (quilt top, batting, and backing,) layered and basted together, ready for quilting.

Quilting The process of stitching through all three layers of the quilt sandwich to secure them and add texture or design.

Selvage The tightly woven, non-fraying edges of a fabric that run along both sides of the width of fabric. Selvages often include printed information such as the fabric designer, collection name, and color swatches.

Width of Fabric (WOF) The measurement of the fabric from one selvage edge to the other, typically 42″–44″ for quilting cotton. In this book, WOF is assumed to be 42″.

Subcut When following pattern instructions, making additional cuts to a previously cut strip or shape.

CUTTING WITH TEMPLATES

This book includes templates for cutting curves. Access the templates by going to Templates (page 124).

If you're using the downloadable PDF, print the templates at 100% scale, and verify that the test square is the correct size. All templates included in this book provide generous trimming allowances to support learning and practice. As you gain confidence and explore patterns beyond this book, please keep in mind that most patterns may not include the same level of flexibility for trimming.

To make the most of the fabric when cutting templates, use the cutting diagrams provided in each project. If you prefer, trace the templates with a fabric marker first. Or, consider making the template from a sturdier cardstock or cardboard so it lasts for multiple uses. Using a smaller rotary cutter, like a 28mm, can help make cutting curved templates easier.

COMMON QUILT BUILDING BLOCKS

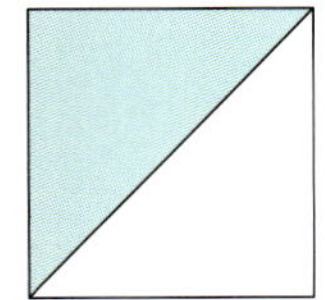

Half-Square Triangles (HSTs) are square blocks split with a diagonal seam.

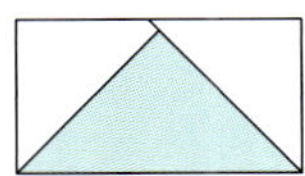

Flying Geese are rectangle blocks with a central triangle.

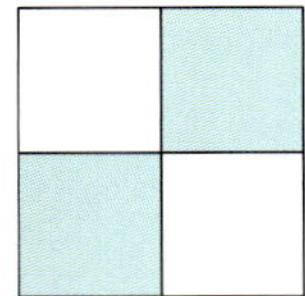

A Four-Patch Block is a square made up of 4 squares in 2 rows.

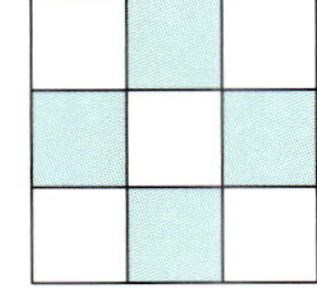

A Nine-Patch Block is a square made up of 9 squares in 3 rows.

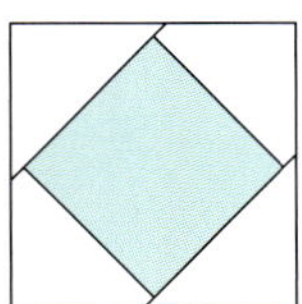

A Square-in-a-Square Block is a quilt block with a smaller square set on point inside a larger square.

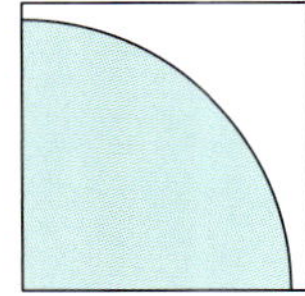

A Quarter-Circle Block is a quilt block made by sewing a curved quarter-circle into the corner of a square.

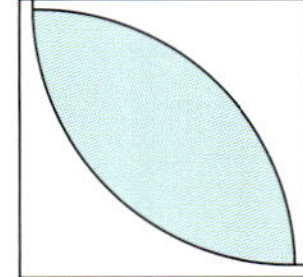

An Orange Peel Block is a quilt block with a petal or eye-shaped curve placed across a square, forming a floral or geometric look.

SEWING STANDARDS

All seam allowances in this book are ¼″. Even if you're more comfortable with using the metric system, stick with imperial measurements (inches) while quilting. Trust me; it'll save you the headache! Using a precise ¼″ seam allowance is crucial. Using a ¼″ foot is the easiest way to make this process simple.

To check if you're sewing with a precise and accurate ¼″ seam allowance:

1. Cut 2 small squares of fabric 2″ × 2″.

2. Sew the 2 squares together along 1 side with a ¼″ seam allowance, aligning the edge of the fabric with the edge of the ¼″ foot. Press the seam to either side (see Pressing, page 20).

3. Measure the new unit. It should measure 2″ × 3½″.

If the measurement across the squares is less than 3½″, your seam is too wide. If the measurement is more than 3½″, your seam is too narrow. Using a ¼″ presser foot can make it much easier to stay consistent, and remember that accurate cutting and careful pressing also play a big part in getting the right measurement. Try again, or you may need to adjust your sewing machine's needle position or guide. Many machines allow you to move the needle slightly to the left or right. If your machine doesn't have that option, try adding a seam guide or a strip of washi tape to your machine as a handy guide for keeping your seams consistent.

Pressing

Pressing is a key step to piecing quilt blocks. The pressing motion for quilting is different from ironing for clothing. Pressing requires a careful, gentle approach that prevents stretching or distorting the fabric. Set the iron down directly on a seam, then pick it straight back up without using a back-and-forth or circular motion against the fabric.

The projects may direct you to press the seams to one side or to press the seams open. When pressing to one side, set the iron down against (next to) the seam. Then, fold the seam to the desired side and press with the iron. When pressing the seam open, run your finger in between the two layers of the seam allowance to open them, then press with the iron.

Chain Piecing

If you've never tried chain piecing before, you're in for a time-saving treat. Chain piecing is a method of sewing your pieces together in a continuous line, one right after the other, without stopping to cut the thread in between. It not only saves time but also conserves thread and keeps your pieces in order.

To chain piece:

1. Stack your units next to your sewing machine in the order you want to sew them.

2. Feed the first pair of fabric pieces through your machine, right sides together, using a consistent ¼˝ seam allowance.

3. Without cutting the thread, feed the next pair of fabric pieces right behind the first.

4. Continue sewing all your pairs this way to create a little chain of sewn units connected by threads.

5. When you're done, snip the threads between the units. Using the thread cutter can help you move through this step even faster.

Chain piecing is especially helpful when you're making a lot of the same unit, like Half-Square Triangles (HSTs) or Flying Geese. I use this method all the time to keep my sewing rhythm going and my blocks nice and consistent.

Trimming

You will often need to trim blocks to match the correct dimensions in the pattern. This ensures that your blocks will fit together properly. Taking a little extra time to trim with care really pays off!

TRIMMING HSTS WITH A SQUARE RULER

1. Position the square ruler over the HST on the cutting mat, aligning the diagonal line of the ruler with the seam of the HST. Ensure the edges of the HST extend slightly beyond the size you need (in this case 4½˝).

2. Trim one side of the HST to square it up. Rotate the HST 90-degrees and trim the next side. Repeat to trim the remaining sides.

TRIMMING HST WITH A SLOTTED TRIMMER RULER

1. Place the unpressed HST on the cutting mat. Position the slotted trimmer ruler over the HST, aligning the dash line of the ruler for the size you need (4½˝) with the sewn line.

2. Cut along both sides of the triangle, keeping the seam lined up with the ruler. The Slotted Trimmer is designed so you can trim both sides without rotating the block. Use the small slots to trim away the dog ears, then press the seams as desired.

TRIMMING FLYING GEESE WITH A SQUARE RULER

Before trimming, ensure that you have a ¼˝ seam allowance at the tip of the triangle to avoid losing the point. In this example, trim to 4½˝ × 8½˝.

1. Place the pressed Flying Geese unit on the cutting mat. Line up the diagonal line of the ruler with the seam line of the unit.

2. Line up the tip of the triangle at 4¼˝ inches (centered) on the ruler.

3. Trim along the right and top sides of the ruler. Carefully rotate the unit and trim the remaining 2 sides.

TRIMMING A SQUARE-IN-A-SQUARE BLOCK

Before trimming, ensure that you have a ¼˝ seam allowance on all four sides at the points of the square. In this example, trim to 5½˝ × 5½˝.

1. On the cutting mat, align one point of the inner square with the 2¾˝ mark (centered) on the ruler.

2. Trim the outer edges of the block, rotating to reach each side and making sure to keep the ¼˝ seam allowance at the tips of the inner square.

TRIMMING A QUARTER-CIRCLE BLOCK AND AN ORANGE PEEL BLOCK

Trimming both of these blocks follows the same process. Before trimming, ensure that you have at least a ¼˝ seam allowance past the curves on all sides.

1. Place the ruler so it is ¼˝ from the seam line on 2 sides. Carefully trim the block's outer edges, preserving the ¼˝ seam allowance.

2. Rotate the block and trim the remaining sides.

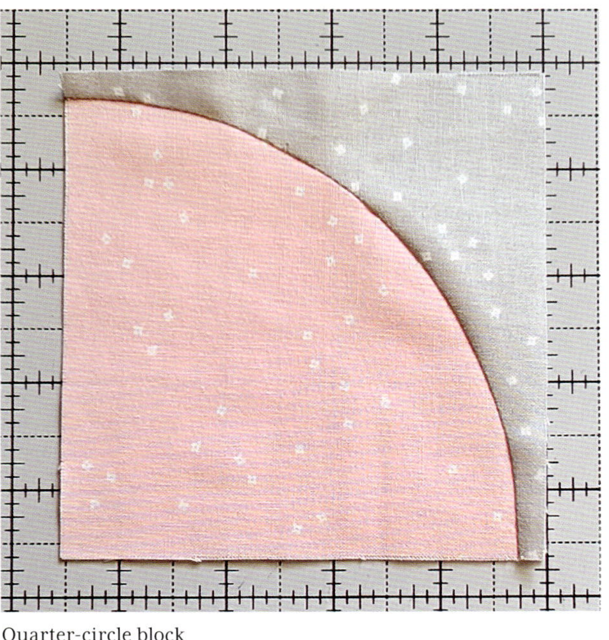

Quarter-circle block

Orange peel block

QUILT ASSEMBLY

Prepare the Layers

If you are spray basting (below), spray the layers as you go.

Backing: Lay the backing fabric wrong side up on a large, flat surface (like the floor). Make sure the backing is at least 8″ wider and longer than the quilt top (4″ on each side). Smooth out any wrinkles and secure the edges to the flat surface with painter's tape, clamps, or weights.

Batting: Place a piece of batting of the same size on top of the backing. Smooth it out so it's evenly spread without any lumps or folds.

Quilt Top: Position the quilt top right side up over the batting, making sure it's centered and there's an equal overhang of batting and backing on all four sides. Smooth everything out so it's wrinkle-free.

Secure the Layers

Choose your preferred basting method, and baste all 3 layers together:

Basting Spray: Lightly spray each layer with basting spray as you layer them together and smooth them out. This is my go-to for quilting with my domestic machine because it's fast and holds everything in place without pinning.

Safety Pins: Pin through all three prepared layers, spacing the pins about 3″–4″ apart. Start from the center and work outward to prevent any shifting of the layers. This method works well for hand quilting and provides a solid hold. As you quilt, remove the pins.

Machine Basting: Machine baste the layers together using a long stitch on a standard sewing machine. This method is quick and effective, especially for smaller quilts or when you want extra hold, though it can be tricky to keep all three layers aligned, and the basting lines can visually distract while you're quilting.

Quilting

Whether you choose to finish your quilt by hand, on your domestic machine, or with a longarm machine, the joy of seeing your quilt come together is unmatched. I have a special place in my heart for hand-quilting, but each method has its own charm and advantages.

TIPS FOR HAND QUILTING

- Choose the right needle and thread. My favorite combination is Aurifil 8wt thread and a Sashiko needle.
- Try to keep the stitches even in length and spacing.
- Hand quilting can be taxing on your hands, so take breaks to avoid strain. Relax your hands, stretch your fingers, and make sure you're not gripping the needle too tightly.

TIPS FOR DOMESTIC MACHINE QUILTING

- Use a walking foot for even stitching, especially on thicker quilts. It moves the top fabric along with the feed dogs underneath, ensuring the quilt layers stay aligned.
- Take your time to go slow and steady, especially when stitching across thicker areas like seams or bulky fabric.
- If you find your quilt is slipping, try using quilting gloves to help guide the fabric smoothly through the machine.

- Depending on your machine, this method might be trickier if you're quilting anything larger than a throw size quilt (about 75˝ length on any side).

PREPARING FOR LONGARM QUILTING

Each longarm quilter will have specific requirements before you send in a quilt. Make sure to review those before preparing your quilt!

- Make sure the quilt is properly squared up, meaning all four sides are the same length and straight.
- Make sure the batting and backing are at least 8˝ wider and longer than the quilt top (4˝ on each side), or whatever dimensions the quilter specifies.
- If the quilt is directional, be sure to mark the top edge of the quilt top and the backing with a piece of masking tape.
- It can be overwhelming to choose from the many quilting designs available. Some quilters use pantographs, an allover design, while others might stitch custom designs. Don't hesitate to consult with your longarm quilter to help you select the perfect design.

Prepare Binding Strips

This book uses 2¼″ double-fold binding.

1. Cut the binding fabric into 2¼″ × WOF strips. Cut enough strips for the perimeter as directed by the project.

2. Place two strips RST at a 90° angle. Starting at the bottom left corner of the top strip, mark a diagonal line to the top right corner of the bottom strip. Sew along the line. Trim diagonally ¼″ from the seam. Press the seam open. Repeat to join all the strips.

3. Fold and press the long strip in half WST. If needed, trim the edges of the strip so they are even.

Attach Binding to the Quilt

1. Align the raw edges of the binding with the raw edges of the quilt. Leaving a 10˝ tail at the beginning, start stitching in the middle of one side of the quilt. Sew it to the front of the quilt with a ¼˝ seam allowance. Stop ¼˝ from the first corner, and backstitch.

2. Remove the quilt from the sewing machine. Fold the binding upward with a 45-degree angle fold.

3. Fold the binding back down, aligning the fold with the raw edge. Starting on the new (perpendicular) edge, continue sewing the binding to the quilt top with a ¼˝ seam allowance.

4. Sew around the entire quilt, repeating Steps 2–3 at each corner, until you are 8˝–10˝ from the starting point. Backstitch, and remove the quilt from the sewing machine.

Finish the Binding Ends

1. Lay the quilt on a flat surface with the right side facing up. Place the starting tail of the binding along the edge of the quilt.

2. Overlap the ending tail of the binding on top of the starting tail Mark the ending tail ½˝ past the end of the starting tail then cut along the marked line.

3. Keeping the binding away from the quilt, sew the two ends together RST with a ¼˝ seam allowance. Press the seam open.

4. Fold the binding in half, wrong sides together. Line up the binding with the edge and attach the remaining binding to the quilt.

5. Fold the binding over the raw quilt edges to the back of the quilt. Give it a good press. Machine or hand stitch it in place to finish.

NOTE

If you are going to machine stitch the binding in place in Step 5, you may want to consider attaching the binding to the back of the quilt first (in Attach Binding to Quilt, page 29*). Doing so means you will fold the binding to the front of the quilt in Step 5, making sure the finishing topstitching on the front is as neat as possible.*

FINISHING WALL HANGINGS

Adding corner sleeves is an easy way to turn your quilt into a wall hanging. These little pockets on the back make it simple to slide in a dowel or rod for hanging. Follow these steps after making a quilt sandwich and before binding the quilt.

1. Cut 2 squares 5″ × 5″ for the corner sleeves. Fold each square in half diagonally to create a triangle. Press the fold to keep it crisp.

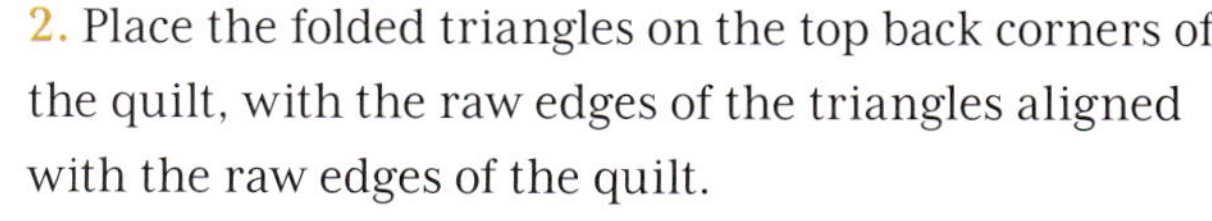

2. Place the folded triangles on the top back corners of the quilt, with the raw edges of the triangles aligned with the raw edges of the quilt.

3. Pin or clip the triangles in place to keep them from shifting. Bind as desired to secure the triangles.

Quilt PROJECTS

Stepping Stones Quilt

The Stepping Stones Quilt focuses on mastering Half-Square Triangles (HSTs). They are such a versatile building block that appear in many quilt designs. You can also sew multiple at once for efficiency. While you can sew up to 8-at-a-time, this book exclusively uses the 2-at-a-time method for simplicity and precision.

This quilt was inspired by colorful stepping stones scattered across a garden path. They may seem randomly placed, but they blend beautifully into the surrounding nature. While the inspiration feels organic and spontaneous, the quilt design itself is structured and balanced, giving your creative choices a strong foundation.

FABRIC

Yardages are based on 42″-wide fabric. Fat Quarter measures (FQ) 18″ × 21″. Fat Eighth (F8) measures 9″ × 21″. I suggest using 18 unique fat quarters or fat eighths for the accent fabrics. To form the groups, split the 18 individual prints into trios. Then divide each trio between accent fabric groups C, D, and E.

There's something refreshing about letting loose with color. Try not to be too strict or afraid to mix a wide range of prints. Let your creativity flow. The best surprises often happen when you trust your instincts. There's also a second version pictured at the end of the chapter with printed fabrics in a more scrappy style. It offers a completely different look with a pieced-together charm, perfect for showing off your favorite stash finds or leftover bits. It's a reminder that even with the same pattern, each quilt can tell its own story.

Fabric A: 2⅞ yards

Fabric B: 1¼ yards

Accent Fabric Group C: 6 FQs

Accent Fabric Group D: 6 F8s

Accent Fabric Group E: 6 F8s

Binding: ⅝ yard

Backing: 4½ yards

Batting: 80″ × 80″

Fabric (Solids)

For this quilt, I used Riley Blake Confetti Cotton in Apricot Blush, Pink Dogwood, Rainforest, Nutmeg, Burnt Orange, Cranberry, Lipstick, Hibiscus, Riley Raspberry, Beach, Milk Can, Canary, Tangerine, Scuba, Sea Glass, Butterscotch, Mellow Rose, Spring Green, Cloud, and Raisin.

Fabric (Prints)

For this quilt, I used Riley Blake A Walk on the Prairie in Silhouette Coral, Sage Gray, Ditsy Sage Gray, Off White, Canyon Rose, Gingham Deep River, Dusty Rose, Floral Sage Gray, Deep River, Dots Marsala, Main Cream, Sage Gray, Wheat Dusty Pink, Stripes Deep River, The Old Garden Emily Marsala, Swiss Dot On White Black, Wanderlust Hawthorn Cream, Piece & Plenty Floral Coral.

Finished Project: 72˝ × 72˝

Skill Level: Advanced Beginner

Pre-Cut Friendly!

Skill Builder: Sewing Half-Square Triangles

CUTTING

This quilt has 6 sections (Q1–Q6). I suggest using swatches to keep track of your fabrics and groups.

Fabric A (Cloud)

Cut 8 strips 4˝ × WOF, subcut into:

- **A1:** 72 squares 4˝ × 4˝

Cut 18 strips 3½˝ × WOF, subcut into:

- **A2:** 216 squares 3½˝ × 3½˝

Fabric B (Raisin)

Cut 4 strips 4˝ × WOF, subcut into:

- **B1:** 36 squares 4˝ × 4˝

Cut 6 strips 3½˝ × WOF, subcut into:

- **B2:** 72 squares 3½˝ × 3½˝

Accent Fabric Group C

Cut from each of 6 FQs:

- **C1:** 12 squares 4˝ × 4˝

Accent Fabric Group D

Cut from each of 6 F8s:

- **D1:** 9 squares 4˝ × 4˝

Accent Fabric Group E

Cut from each of 6 F8s:

- **E1:** 9 squares 4˝ × 4˝

Binding

Cut 8 strips 2¼˝ × WOF.

FABRIC			
A		B	
Section	Accent Group C	Accent Group D	Accent Group E
Q1			
Q2			
Q3			
Q4			
Q5			
Q6			

CONSTRUCTION

Press all the seams open unless otherwise noted. Keep the HST Units organized by Section (Q1–Q6) to avoid confusion when assembling.

How to Make 2-At-a-Time HSTs

This method yields 2 identical HSTs.

1. Choose 2 squares of the same size. Draw a diagonal line from corner to corner on the wrong side of the lighter colored square. Place the lighter square on top of the darker square. Sew a ¼˝ seam on both sides of the drawn line. *fig. A*

2. Cut on the drawn line. *fig. B*

3. Press the seams, and trim to size. *fig. C*

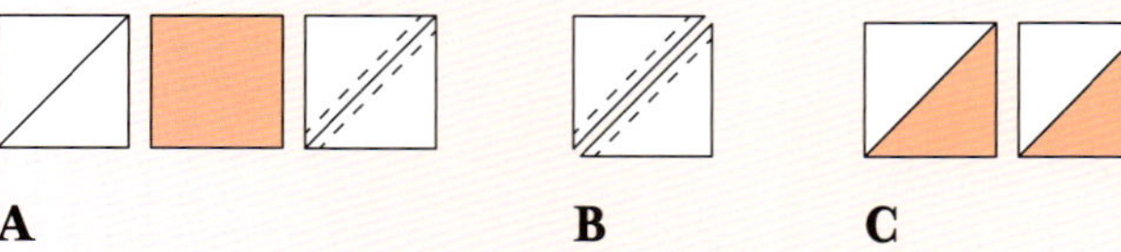

Make HST Units

Sew the HST Units together using the 2-At-a-Time method. Pair 2 squares together as listed below to make the required number of HSTs. Press and trim all HSTs to 3½″ × 3½″.

Pair 36 A1 squares with 36 C1 squares, using 6 C1 squares of each color. You will have 12 A1C1 HST Units in each colorway. ***fig. A***

Pair 36 A1 squares with 36 D1 squares, using 6 D1 squares of each color. You will have 12 A1D1 HST Units in each colorway. ***fig. B***

Pair 36 B1 squares with 36 E1 squares, using 6 E1 squares of each color. You will have 12 B1E1 HST Units in each colorway. ***fig. C***

Pair 18 C1 squares with 18 D1 squares, using 3 C1 squares and 3 D1 squares of each color. You will have 6 C1D1 HST Units in each colorway. ***fig. D***

Pair 18 C1 squares with 18 E1 squares, using 3 C1 squares and 3 E1 squares from each color. You will have 6 C1E1 HST Units in each colorway. ***fig. E***

A

B

C

D

E

Make Sections

1. To make a Section, arrange the units into 4 rows as shown. Pay close attention to the orientation of the HST Units. ***fig. F***

Row 1: C1D1 HST, A1D1 HST, A2 square, B1E1 HST

Row 2: A1D1 HST, A2 square, B2 square, A2 square

Row 3: A2 square, B2 square, A2 square, A1C1 HST

Row 4: B1E1 HST, A2 square, A1C1 HST, C1E1 HST

2. Sew the units into rows, and press. ***fig. G***

3. Sew the rows together, and press. This is Section 1 (Q1). If needed, trim to 12½″ × 12½″. Repeat to make a total of 6 Q1 Units. ***fig. H***

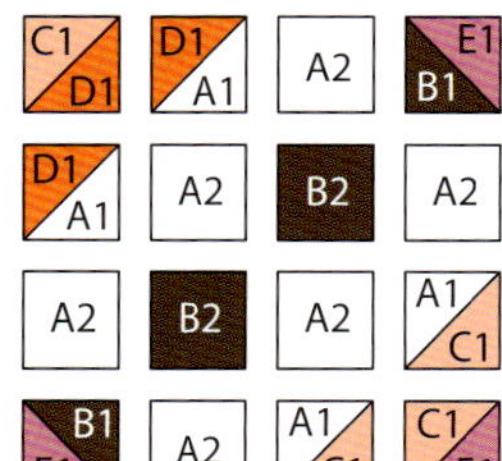

F

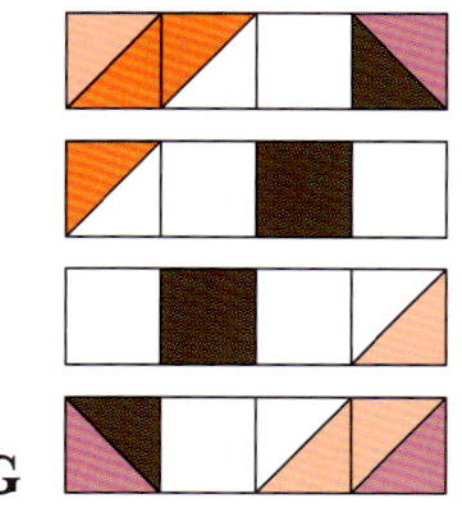

G

H

Make 6 Q1 Units.

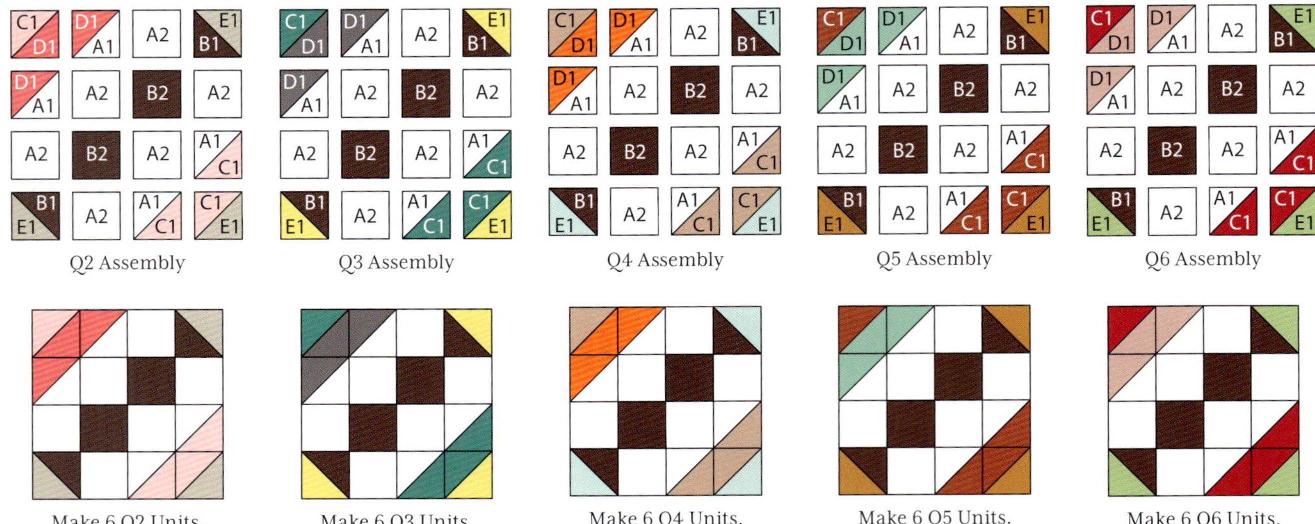

Make 6 Q2 Units. Make 6 Q3 Units. Make 6 Q4 Units. Make 6 Q5 Units. Make 6 Q6 Units.

I

4. Repeat Steps 1–3 to make 6 units each of Q2–Q6. ***fig. I***

Assemble the Blocks

1. To make Block 1, arrange 4 units into 2 rows as shown. Pay close attention to the orientation of each unit: ***fig. J***

   Row 1: Q1 Unit, Q6 Unit

   Row 2: Q2 Unit, Q4 Unit

2. Sew the units into rows, and press. ***fig. K***

3. Sew the rows together, and press. Repeat to make a total of 3 Block 1s. If needed, trim to 24½″ × 24½″. ***fig. L***

4. Repeat Steps 1–3 to arrange and sew Block 2 as shown. Make a total of 3 Block 2s. If needed, trim to 24½″ × 24½″. ***fig. M***

   Row 1: Q3 Unit, Q1 Unit

   Row 2: Q5 Unit, Q6 Unit

5. Repeat Steps 1–3 to arrange and sew Block 3 as shown. Make a total of 3 Block 3s. If needed, trim to 24½″ × 24½″. ***fig. N***

   Row 1: Q4 Unit, Q5 Unit

   Row 2: Q2 Unit, Q3 Unit

J **K**

L

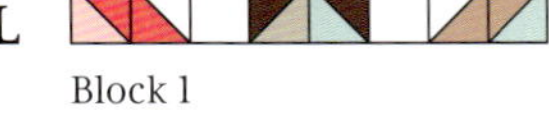

Block 1

M

Block 2

N

Block 3

O **P**

Assemble the Quilt

1. Arrange Blocks into 3 rows as shown. Sew the units into rows and press. ***fig. O***

   Row 1: Block 2, Block 3, Block 1

   Row 2: Block 1, Block 3, Block 2

   Row 3: Block 3, Block 2, Block 1

2. Sew the units into rows and press. Sew the rows together, and press. The quilt top measures 72½″ × 72½″. ***fig. P***

Finish the Quilt

Layer, quilt, and bind the project as desired. See Quilt Assembly (page 24).

Gemstone Path Quilt

The Gemstone Path quilt uses the stitch-and-flip (SNF) piecing method, making this design come together with crisp, clean lines that mimic the sparkle of gemstone facets. Whether you love bold, vibrant colors or prefer soft, muted tones, this quilt is a great way to show off your favorite fabrics.

Using the SNF Method

Stitch-and-flip piecing allows you to sew unique shapes and units without having to cut complicated triangles or irregular geometric shapes. It does involve some fabric waste, but it's the best way to achieve many of these shapes. Once you start using this method, refer back to these tips for easy piecing:

- You'll often be directed to sew on a marked line. Instead of sewing directly on the marked line, stitch a thread-width closer to the edge that will be trimmed. This keeps the finished unit the correct size.
- Make sure the corner you're "flipping" is oriented the correct way.
- Chain piece to save time.

FABRIC

Yardages are based on 42″-wide fabric. Fat Quarter (FQ) measures 18″ × 21″.

Fabric A: 1⅞ yards

Accent Fabric: 16 FQs

Sashing: ¾ yard

Binding: ½ yard

Backing: 4¼ yard

Batting: 74″ × 74″

Fabric

For this quilt, I used Riley Blake Confetti Cottons in Dove, Hint of Mint, Jazzberry, Frosting, Sunset, Pumpkin, Sea Glass, Cadet, Pink Dogwood, Tea Rose, Grass, Curry, Canary, Cinnamon, Mellow Rose, Le Creme, and Pewter.

Finished Project: 66″ × 66″
Skill Level: Beginner
Pre-Cut Friendly!
Skill Builder: Sewing Stitch and Flip Units

CUTTING

Fabric A (Le Creme)

Cut 3 strips 6½″ × WOF, subcut into:

- **A1:** 16 squares 6½″ × 6½″
- **A2:** 4 squares 3½″ × 3½″

Cut 5 strips 3½″ × WOF, subcut into:

- **A2:** 60 squares 3½″ × 3½″ (total of 64)

Cut 12 strips 2″ × WOF, subcut into:

- **A3:** 252 squares 2″ × 2″

Cut 1 strip 2½″ × WOF, subcut into:

- **A4:** 9 squares 2½″ × 2½″
- **A3:** 4 squares 2″ × 2″ (total of 256)

Accent Fabric

From each of the 16 FQs:

Cut 4 strips 3½″ × length of FQ, subcut into:

- **B1:** 8 rectangles 3½″ × 5″
- **B2:** 1 rectangle 3½″ × 8½″
- **B4:** 4 squares 2″ × 2″

Cut 1 strip 2″ × length of FQ, subcut into:

- **B3:** 2 rectangles 2″ × 8½″

Sashing Fabric (Pewter)

Cut 1 strip 15½″ × WOF, subcut into:

- **C1:** 16 rectangles 2½″ × 15½″

Cut 4 strips 2½″ × WOF, subcut into:

- **C1:** 8 rectangles 2½″ × 15½″

Binding

Cut into 7 strips 2¼″ × width of fabric (WOF).

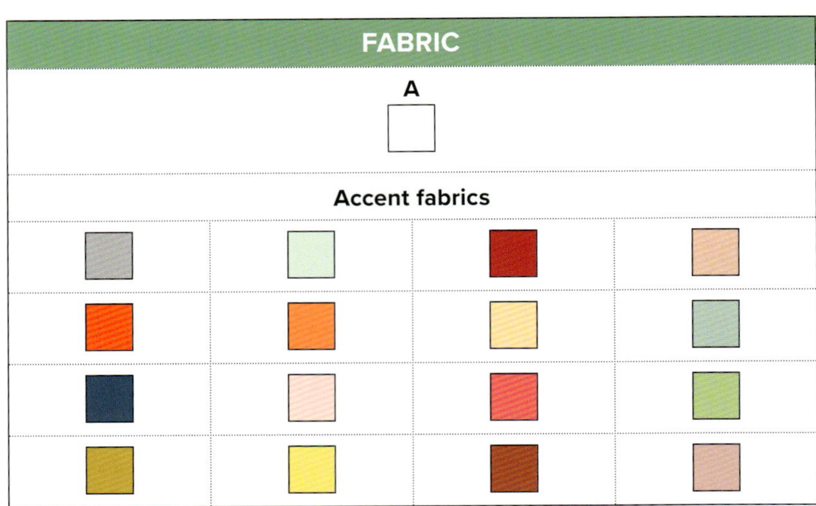

CONSTRUCTION

Block Overview

The Gemstone Path Quilt is composed of Block A and Block B. Block B mirrors Block A. Each block includes 4 accent fabrics. Each group of 4 accent fabrics will result in 2 blocks. So, divide the 16 accent fabrics into 4 groups of 4, then assign each fabric a label FQ1–FQ4 within each group. I recommend mixing and arranging all the pieces for each block before you begin sewing.

Each Gemstone A Block needs the following pieces ***(fig. A)***:

- 1 A1 square
- 4 A2 squares
- 16 A3 squares
- 4 B1 rectangles from (FQ1-B1)
- 4 B1 rectangles from (FQ2-B1)
- 1 B2 rectangle from FQ3 (FQ3-B2)
- 4 B4 squares from FQ3 (FQ3-B4)
- 2 B3 rectangles from FQ4 (FQ4-B3)

Each Gemstone B Block needs the following pieces ***(fig. B)***:

- 1 A1 square
- 4 A2 squares
- 16 A3 squares
- 4 B1 rectangles from (FQ1-B1)
- 4 B1 rectangles from (FQ2-B1)
- 1 B2 rectangle from FQ4 (FQ4-B2)
- 4 B4 squares from FQ4 (FQ4-B4)
- 2 B3 rectangles from FQ3 (FQ3-B3)

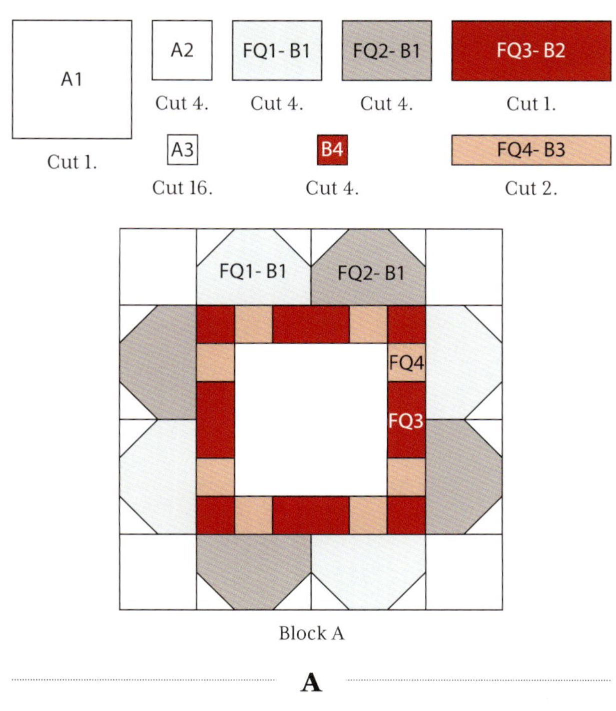

Block A

A

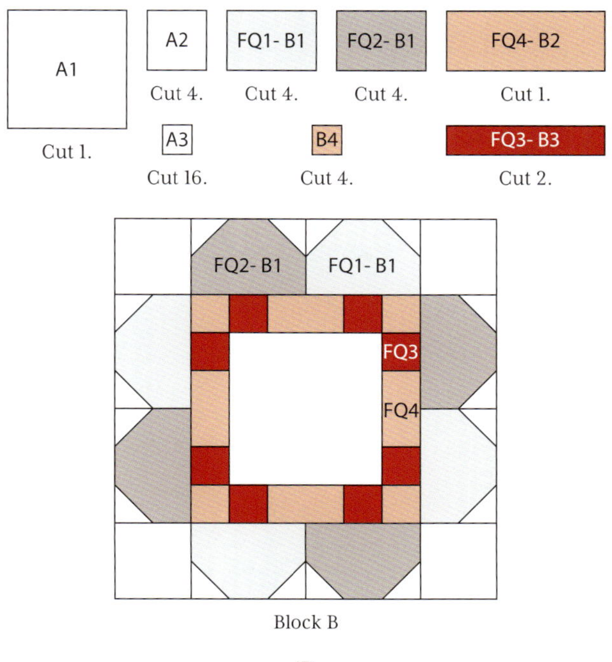

Block B

B

Gem Petal Units

1. Draw a diagonal line on the wrong side of all A3 squares. Place 2 A3 squares on the top corners of an FQ1-B1 rectangle, RST with the lines oriented as shown. Sew on the lines, then trim off the corners ¼″ away from the seams. ***fig. C***

2. Flip the A3 corner pieces away from the FQ1-B1 piece, and press the seams open. ***fig. D***

3. Repeat Steps 1–2 with all of A3 squares and B1 rectangles to make the following SNF Units. You will have 8 SNF Units from each accent color (4 for Block As used in Step 4, and 4 for Block Bs used in Step 5). ***fig. E***

4. Sew 2 SNF Units together per your block arrangement to make one Gem Petal unit A (GP-A). Press the seam open. Repeat to make a total of 4 GP-A units from each pair of SNF units. Set aside for Block As. ***fig. F***

5. Repeat Step 4 to sew Gem Petal unit Bs (GP-Bs). Mirror the color placement of the GP-A units. Set aside for Block Bs. ***fig. G***

C **D** **E**

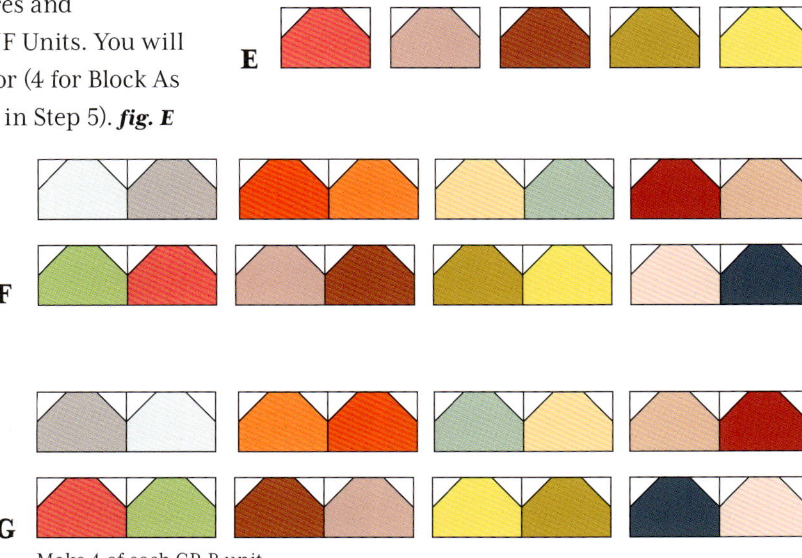

Make 4 of each GP-B unit.

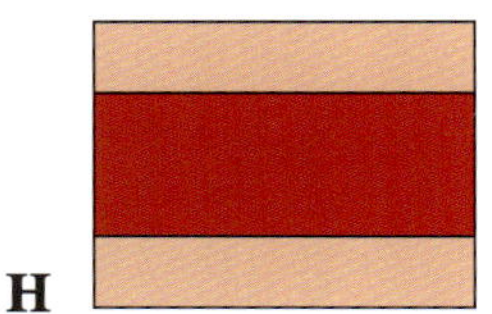
H

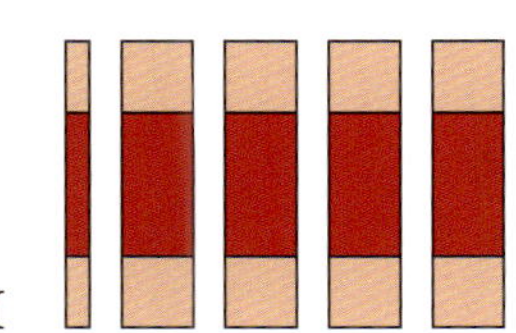
I

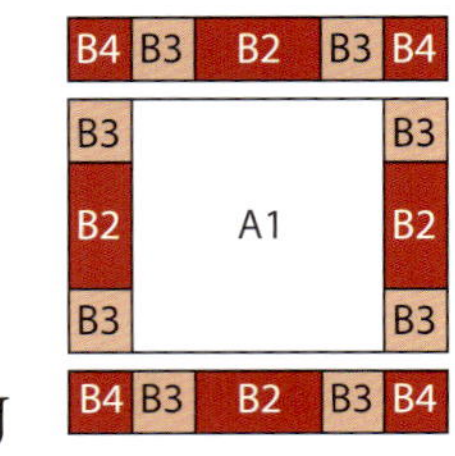

J

K

Block A Center Units

Use a smaller stitch length for strip piecing. My preference is 1.9–2mm.

1. Arrange the rectangles into rows, and sew them together. Press the seams toward the center. ***fig. H***

   Row 1: FQ4-B3 Rectangle

   Row 2: FQ3-B2 Rectangle

   Row 3: FQ4-B3 Rectangle

2. Cut the Step 1 unit into 4 rectangles 2˝ × 6½˝. Call each unit Gem Tile Strip A (GT-A). ***fig. I***

3. Arrange the following units into rows, and sew them together. Press the seams away from the GT-A units. ***fig. J***

   Row 1: FQ3-B4 square, Unit GT-A, FQ3-B4 square

   Row 2: Unit GT-A, A1 square, Unit GT-A

   Row 3: FQ3-B4 square, Unit GT-A, FQ3-B4 square

L

4. Sew the rows together, and press the seams open. Call this Center Unit A. ***fig. K***

5. Repeat Steps 1–4 to make 7 more Center Unit As. ***fig. L***

Block B Center Units

Use a smaller stitch length for strip piecing. My preference is 1.9–2mm.

1. Arrange the rectangles into rows, and sew them together. Press the seams toward the center. ***fig. M***

   Row 1: FQ3-B3 Rectangle

   Row 2: FQ4-B2 Rectangle

   Row 3: FQ3-B3 Rectangle

2. Cut the Step 1 unit into 4 rectangles 2˝ × 6½˝. Call each unit Gem Tile Strip B (GT-B). ***fig. N***

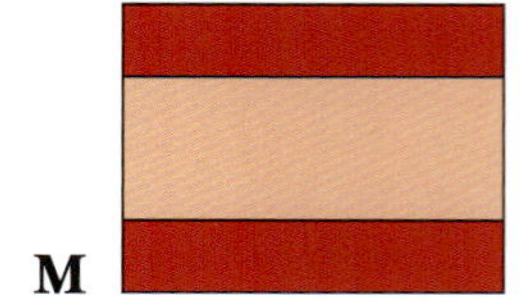
M

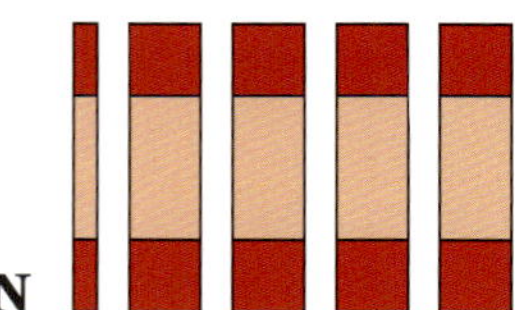
N

3. Arrange the following units into rows, and sew them together. Press the seams away from the GT-B units. ***fig. O***

Row 1: FQ4-B4 square, Unit GT-B, FQ4-B4 square

Row 2: Unit GT-B, A1 square, Unit GT-B

Row 3: FQ4-B4 square, Unit GT-B, FQ4-B4 square

4. Sew the rows together, and press the seams open. Call this Center Unit B. ***fig. P***

5. Repeat Steps 1–4 to make 7 more Center Unit Bs. ***fig. Q***

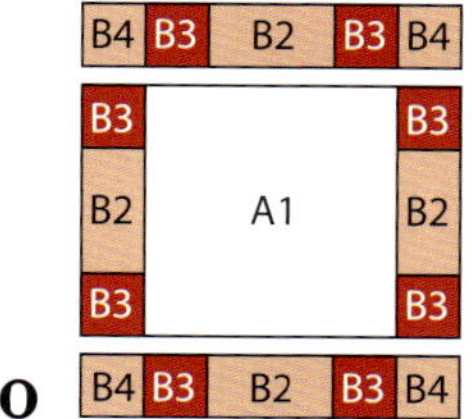

O

P

Q

Make Block A

1. Arrange the following units into 3 rows. ***fig. R***

Row 1: A2 square, Unit GP-A, A2 square

Row 2: Unit GP-A, Center Unit A, Unit GP-A

Row 3: A2 square, Unit GP-A, A2 square

2. Sew the units into rows, then sew the rows together. Press all the seams open. Block A measures 15½″ × 15½″. ***fig. S***

3. Repeat Steps 1–2 to make 7 more Block As. ***fig. T***

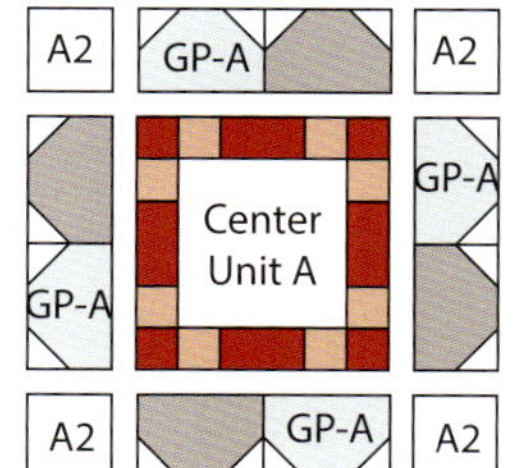

R

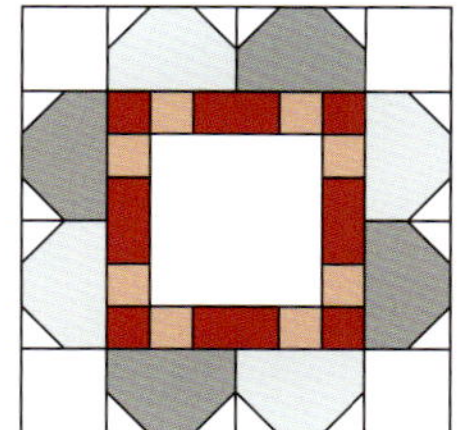

S

T

Make Block B

1. Arrange the following units into 3 rows. ***fig. U***

   Row 1: A2 square, Unit GP-B, A2 square

   Row 2: Unit GP-B, Center Unit B, Unit GP-B

   Row 3: A2 square, Unit GP-B, A2 square

2. Sew the units into rows, then sew the rows together. Press all the seams open. Block B measures 15½″ × 15½″. ***fig. V***

3. Repeat Steps 1–2 to make 7 more Block B. ***fig. W***

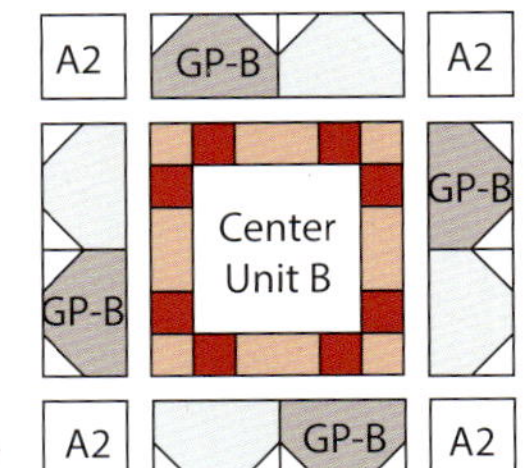

U

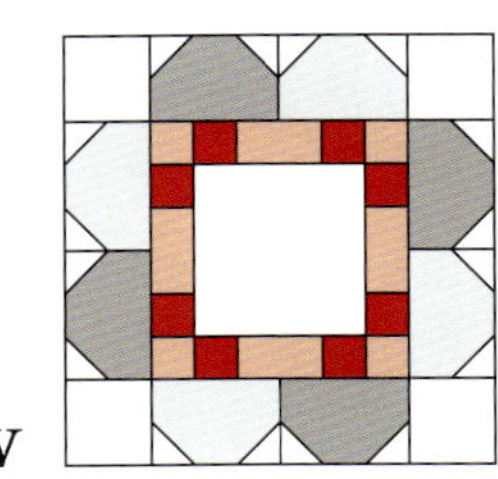

V

W

Assemble the Quilt

1. Arrange Blocks A and B into 4 rows as desired with sashing (C1 rectangles) and cornerstones (A4 squares) as shown. Each Main Row consists of 4 Block A and/or Block B units, alternating with 3 C1 rectangles as shown. The sashing rows consist of 4 C1 rectangles, alternating with 3 A4 squares. ***fig. X***

2. Sew the units into rows. Press the seams toward the sashing. ***fig. Y***

X

Y

Z

3. Sew the rows together. Press the seams toward the sashing. The quilt top measures 66½″ × 66½″. ***fig. Z***

Finish the Quilt

Layer, quilt, and bind the project as desired. See Quilt Assembly (page 24).

Bloomer Quilt

The Bloomer Quilt is all about making curves approachable and fun. The templates are designed with extra wiggle room to make trimming a breeze! The Bloomer Quilt has a fresh, floral feel that often reminds me of springtime, but its design is flexible to take on a completely different mood with seasonal fabrics. With gentle curves and simple HSTs coming together to form each flower-like block, this quilt adds a soft, cheerful touch. It feels as if blossoms are unfolding right on your quilt top, bringing warmth and movement to your space.

Sewing Quarter-Circle Blocks

Sewing curves can be intimidating for quilters, but I promise that with enough pins and generous templates, this will soon be your favorite piecing technique! As you follow the step-by-step instructions, remember these tips:

- Use a smaller 28mm rotary cutter instead of the standard 45mm to avoid odd sharp corners when cutting curves.
- Marking the center of a curve might sound tedious, but it gives you an accurate starting point when pinning, which is crucial for your blocks to turn out just right.
- Pin in three key spots: center, left edge, and right edge. Then, add more pins in between to keep everything aligned.
- Sew slowly and guide the fabric gently without pulling or stretching. Don't be afraid to lift the presser foot to adjust the fabric as you go.
- After sewing the curve, snip small notches into the seam allowance (without cutting through the stitches). This helps release tension and makes the fabric lie flatter when you press it.

FABRIC

Yardages are based on 42˝-wide fabric.

Fabric A: 3 yards

Accent Fabric Group B: ½ yard of 6 colors

Accent Fabric Group C: ½ yard of 6 colors

Fabric D: 10˝ square

Binding: ⅝ yard

Backing: 7¼ yards*

Batting: 86˝ × 86˝

*Note: Backing includes 4˝ overage on each side. If your WOF is 43˝ or wider, you will only need 4⅞ yards of backing.

Fabric (Solids)

For this quilt, I used Riley Blake Dainty Daisy in Songbird, Lilac, Lipstick, Butterscotch, Frosting, Alpine, Gray, Peony, Honey, Jazzberry, On Cloud Vintage Pastels, Confetti Cottons in Tea Dye, and, Cinnamon.

Fabric (Prints)

For this quilt, I used Riley Blake Ski Hill in Main Teal, Main Powder, Main Aqua, Tracks Aqua, Tracks Red, Snowflakes Teal, Sweater White, Magical Winterland Tonal Barn Red, Snowflake Blue, Knitwear Winter, Foliage Blue, Gingham Green, and Blossom in Navy.

Finished Project: 78″ × 78″
Skill Level: Intermediate
Skill Builder: Sewing Quarter-Circles

CUTTING

To access the templates, go to Templates (page 124). For this project, you need Template A and Template B. Refer to the cutting diagrams to most efficiently cut the templates from the fabric.

Fabric A (Cloud Vintage Pastel)

Cut 6 strips 7″ × WOF, subcut into:

- **A1:** 36 squares 7″ × 7″

Cut 5 strips 5¾″ × WOF, subcut into:

- **A2:** 72 Template B

Cut 12 strips 2½″ × WOF, subcut into:

- **A3:** 36 rectangles 2½″ × 12½″

Accent Fabric Group B

From each of the 6 fabrics in Fabric Group B:

Cut 1 strip 7″ × WOF, subcut into:

- **B1:** 3 squares 7″ × 7″
- **B2:** 6 rectangles 6½″ × 2½″

Cut 1 strip 4½″ × WOF, subcut into:

- **B3:** 6 Template A
- **B4:** 6 rectangles 4½″ × 2½″

Accent Fabric Group C

From each of the 6 fabrics in Fabric Group C:

Cut 1 strip 7″ × WOF, subcut into:

- **C1:** 3 squares 7″ × 7″
- **C2:** 6 rectangles 6½″ × 2½″

Cut 1 strip 4½″ × WOF, subcut into:

- **C3:** 6 Template A
- **C4:** 6 rectangles 4½″ × 2½″

FABRIC		
A		D
Colorway	**Accent Group B**	**Accent Group C**
1		
2		
3		
4		
5		
6		

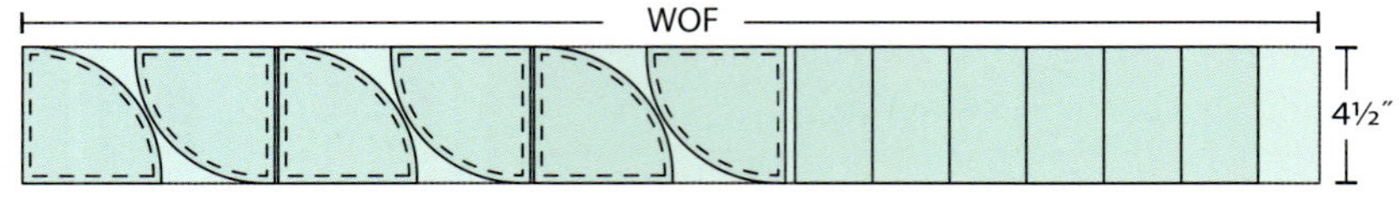

Cutting Template A

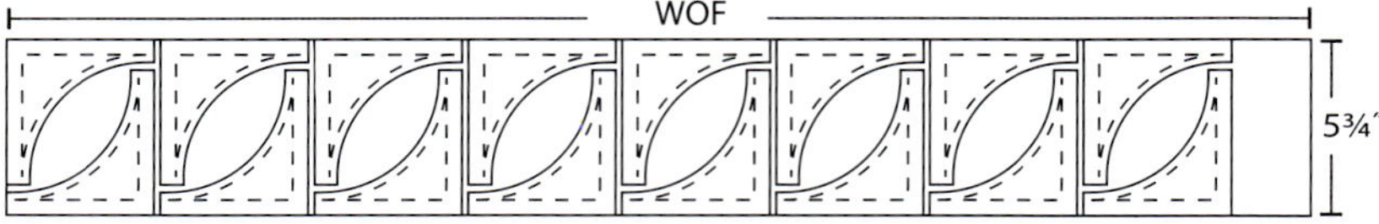

Cutting Template B

Fabric D

D1: Cut 9 squares 2½″ × 2½″

Binding

Cut into 8 strips 2¼″ × width of fabric (WOF).

CONSTRUCTION

Quarter-Circle Blocks

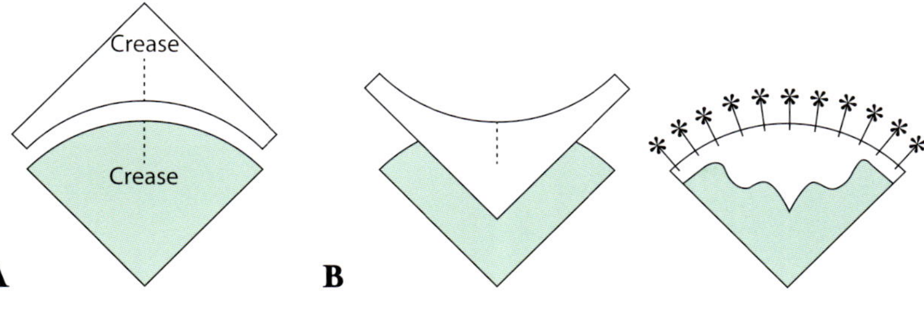

1. Pair an A2 with a B3. Fold each piece in half to crease the centers. ***fig. A***

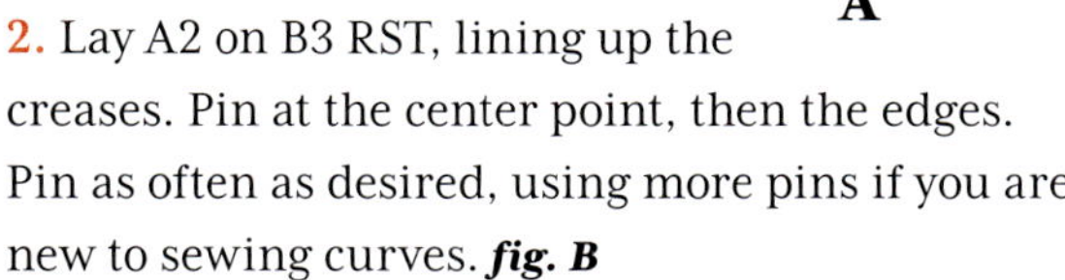

2. Lay A2 on B3 RST, lining up the creases. Pin at the center point, then the edges. Pin as often as desired, using more pins if you are new to sewing curves. ***fig. B***

3. Sew with a ¼″ seam along the curve, carefully adjusting the fabric as needed. ***fig. C***

4. Press the seam toward A2. Trim to 4½″ × 4½″, maintaining a ¼″ seam allowance on both sides of the curve. ***fig. D***

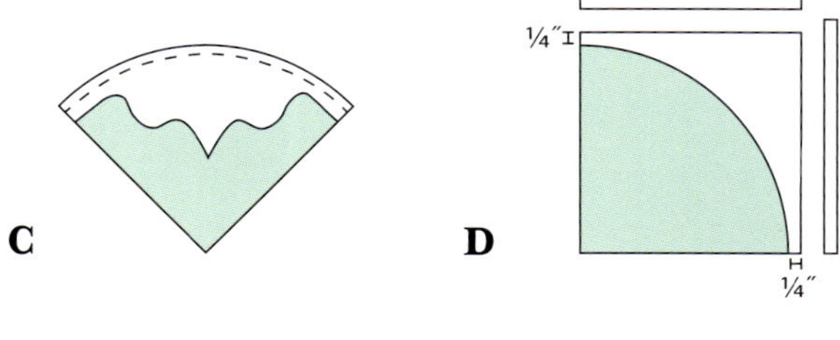

5. Repeat Steps 1–4 pairing the remaining 71 A2 pieces with the 35 B3 pieces and 36 C3 pieces. You will have a total of 36 A2B3 Quarter-Circle Blocks, and 36 A2C3 Quarter-Circle Blocks (6 blocks in each colorway). ***fig. E***

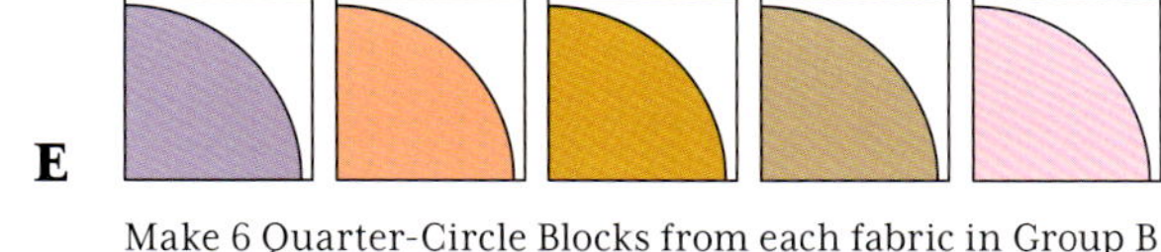

Make 6 Quarter-Circle Blocks from each fabric in Group B.

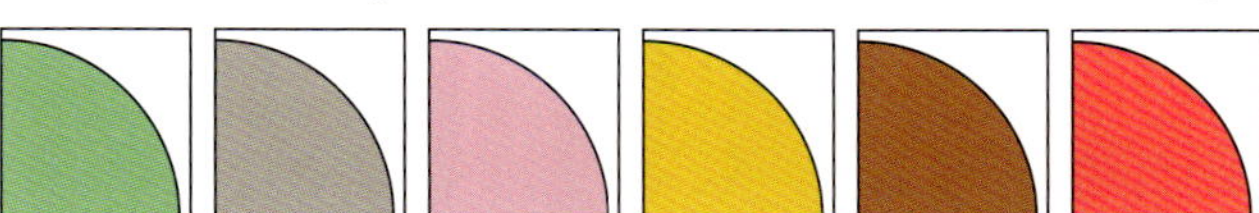

Make 6 Quarter-Circle Blocks from each fabric in Group C.

Half-Square Triangle Units (HST)

1. Draw a diagonal line on the wrong side of all A1 squares. Pair each A1 square with a B1 square. Sew with a ¼″ seam on both sides of the line (see How to Make 2-at-a-time HSTs, page 36). ***fig. F***

2. Cut on the drawn line. Press the seams open, and trim to 6½″ × 6½″. ***fig. G***

3. Repeat Steps 1–2 pairing the 35 remaining A1 squares with the 17 B1 squares and 18 C1 squares. You will make a total of 36 A1B1 HST Blocks, and 36 A1C1 HST Blocks, 6 blocks in each colorway. ***fig. H***

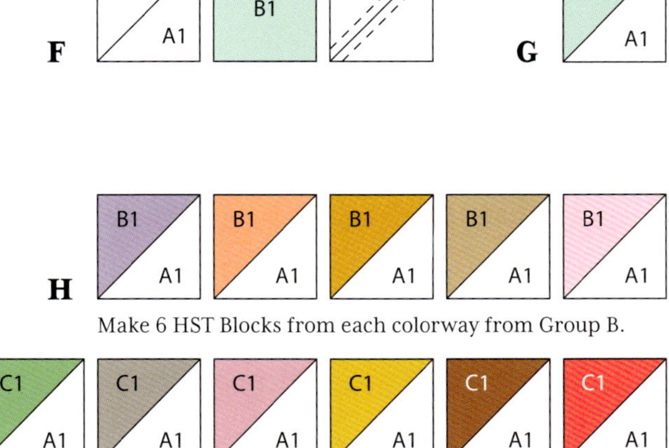

Make 6 HST Blocks from each colorway from Group B.

Make 6 HST Blocks from each colorway from Group C.

Make Unit 1 and Unit 2

1. Sew a B4 rectangle to the left side of a coordinating A2B3 Quarter-Circle Block. Press the seam toward the B4 rectangle. Sew a coordinating B2 rectangle to the top of the unit. Press the seam toward the B2 rectangle. ***fig. I***

2. Sew a coordinating A1B1 HST block to the top of the unit. Press the seam open. Call this Unit 1, measuring 6½″ × 12½″. ***fig. J***

3. Repeat Steps 1–2, pairing the 35 remaining A2B3 Quarter-Circle Blocks with the coordinating B2 and B4 rectangles, and then with the 35 coordinating A1B1 HST Blocks. You will make a total of 36 Unit 1s (6 units from each of 6 colorways in Fabric Group B). ***fig. K***

4. Sew a C4 rectangle to the right side of a coordinating A2C3 Quarter-Circle Block. Press the seam toward the C4 rectangle. Sew a coordinating C2 rectangle to the bottom of the unit. Press the seam toward the C2 rectangle. ***fig. L***

5. Sew a coordinating A1C1 HST block to the bottom of the Step 4 unit. Press the seam open. Call this Unit 2, measuring 6½″ × 12½″. ***fig. M***

6. Repeat Steps 4–5 pairing the 35 remaining A2C3 Quarter-Circle Blocks with the coordinating C2 and C4 rectangles, and then with the 35 coordinating A1C1 HST Blocks. You will make a total of 36 Unit 2s (6 units in each of the 6 colorways in Fabric group C). ***fig. N***

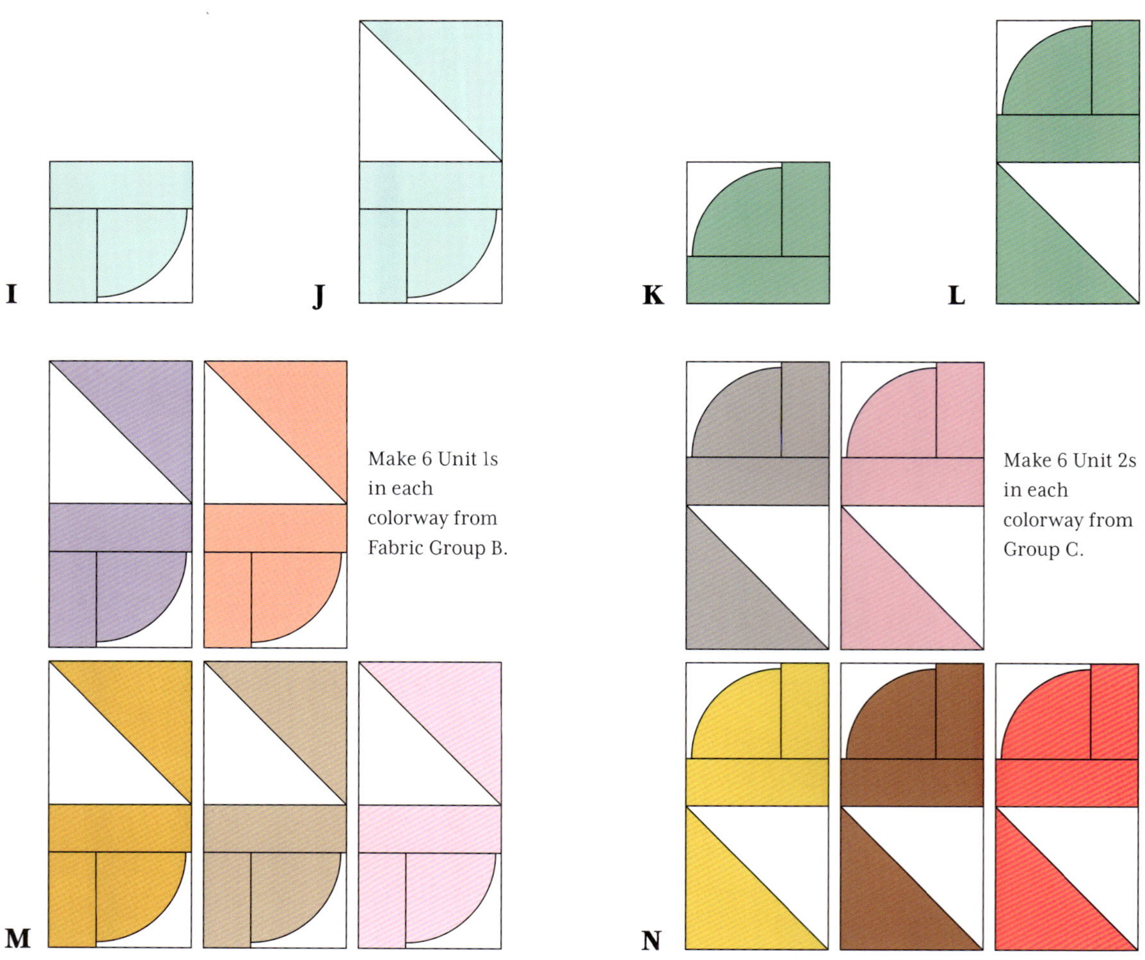

Make Quadrants

1. Pair and sew together a Unit 1 with a Unit 2. Coordinate by matching a Fabric 1 unit from group B with a Fabric 1 unit from Group C, continuing for all fabric numbers. Press the seam open. ***fig. O***

2. Repeat Step 1 with the 35 remaining Unit 1s and Unit 2s to make a total of 36 Quadrants. Each Quadrant measures 12½″ × 12½″. ***fig. P***

Assemble the Blocks

This is the fun part! Mix and match the Quadrants into Blocks, and then lay out the entire quilt before sewing each block together. There are no sashing strips between the blocks. To achieve the same look as the cover quilt, avoid placing Quadrants of the same colorway next to each other. I highly recommend taking your time laying out the Quadrants.

1. Arrange the below units into 3 rows (***fig. Q***):

   Row 1: Quadrant, A3 rectangle, Quadrant

   Row 2: A3 rectangle, D1 square, A3 rectangle

   Row 3: Quadrant, A3 rectangle, Quadrant

2. Sew the units into rows, then sew the rows together. Press the seams open. Each block measures 26½″ × 26½″. ***fig. R***

3. Repeat Steps 1–2 to make a total of 9 Blocks.

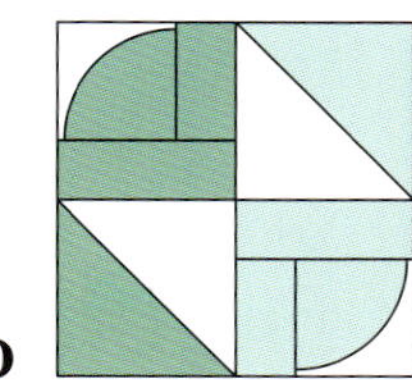

O

Make 6 Quadrants in each of 6 colorways.

P

Q

R

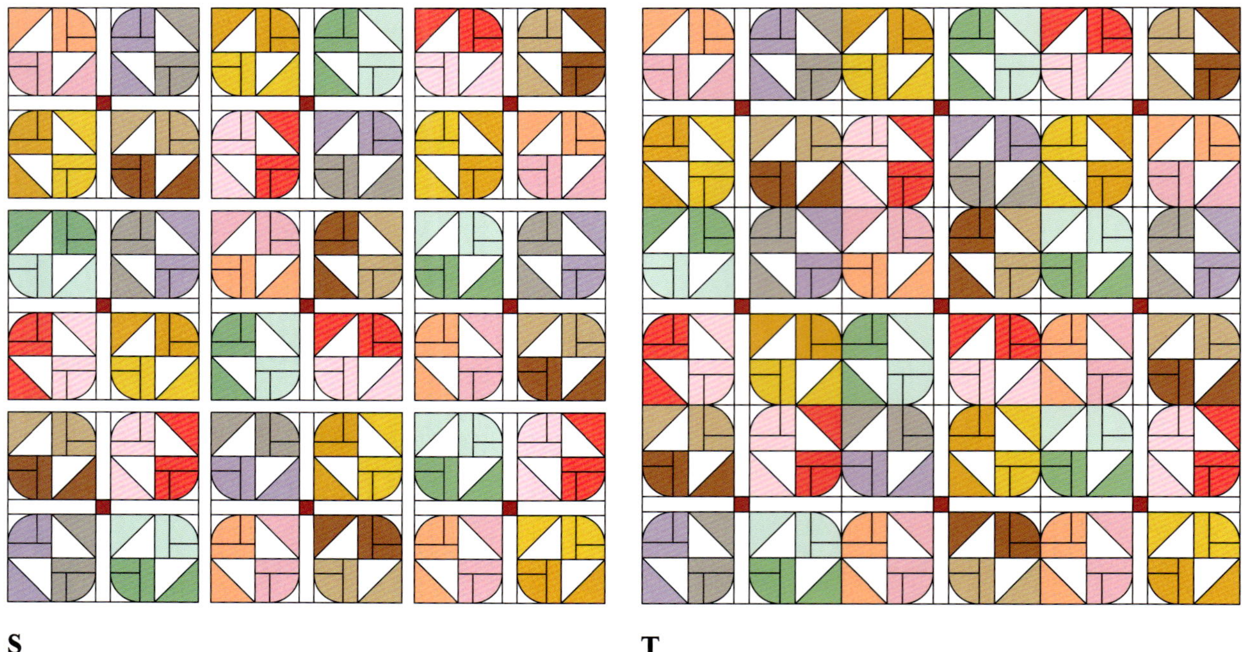

Assemble the Quilt

1. Arrange the blocks into 3 rows, with 3 blocks in each row as shown. ***fig. S***

2. Sew the units into rows, then sew the rows together. Press the seams open. The quilt top measures 78½″ × 78½″. ***fig. T***

Finish the Quilt

Layer, quilt, and bind the project as desired. See Quilt Assembly (page 24).

MINI PROJECT

Fresh Cut Table Runner

This project is pre-cut friendly! Step into spring with this table runner, a design inspired by the crisp, refreshing vibe of new blooms and bright days. This playful yet elegant runner showcases quarter-circle and orange peel blocks, combining their curved beauty to create a flowing, petal-like effect.

MATERIALS

Yardages are based on 42″-wide fabric. Fat Eighth (F8) measures 9″ × 21″.

Fabric A: 1⅛ yard

Fabric B: 1 F8

Fabric C: 1 F8

Fabric D: 1 F8

Fabric E: 1 F8

Fabric F: ½ yard

Binding: ⅓ yard

Backing: 2 yards

Batting: 26″ × 68″

Fabric

For this quilt, I used Riley Blake Confetti Cotton in Sunshine, Petal Pink, Riley Mustard, Riley Raspberry, Alpine, and Cloud.

Finished Project: 18″ × 60″
Skill Level: Intermediate
Skill Builder: Sewing Curves

CUTTING

To access the templates, go to Templates (page 124). For this project, you need Template C, Template D, and Template E.

Fabric A (Cloud)

Cut 3 strips 8¾″ × WOF, subcut into:

- **A1:** 24 Template E

Cut 4 strips 2½″ × WOF, sew 3 together and subcut into:

- **A3:** 2 strips 2½″ × 60½″

From remaining strips, subcut:

- **A2:** 2 strips 2½″ × 14½″

Fabric B (Sunshine)

B1: 2 Template D

Fabric C (Petal Pink)

C1: 2 Template D

Fabric D (Mustard)

D1: 2 Template D

Fabric E (Raspberry)

E1: 2 Template D

Fabric F (Alpine)

Cut 2 strips 7½″ × WOF, subcut into:

- **F1:** 8 Template C

Binding

Cut 4 strips 2¼″ × width of fabric (WOF).

CONSTRUCTION

Seam allowances are ¼″ unless otherwise noted.

Quarter-Circle Blocks

1. Pair an A1 with a B1 pieces. Fold each piece in half to crease the centers. ***fig. A***

2. Lay A1 on B1 RST, lining up the crease lines. Pin at the center point, then the edges. Pin as often as desired, using more pins if you are new to sewing curves. ***fig. B***

3. Sew with a ¼″ seam along the curve, carefully adjusting the fabric as needed. ***fig. C***

4. Press the seam toward A1. Trim to 7½″ × 7½″, maintaining a ¼″ seam allowance on both sides of the curve. Call this Q1. Repeat to make a second Q1. Press the seam for the second unit toward B1. ***fig. D***

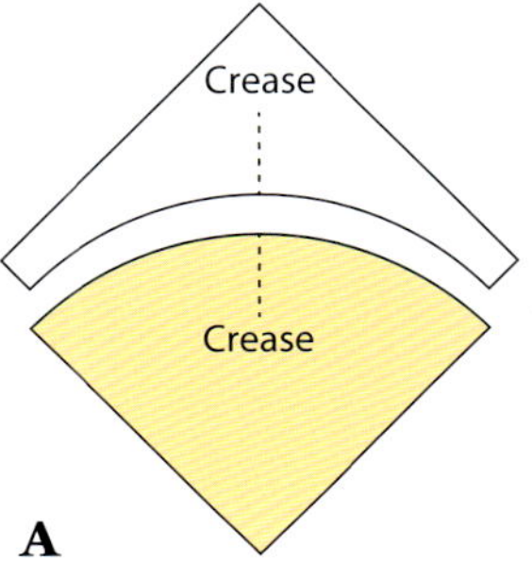

A

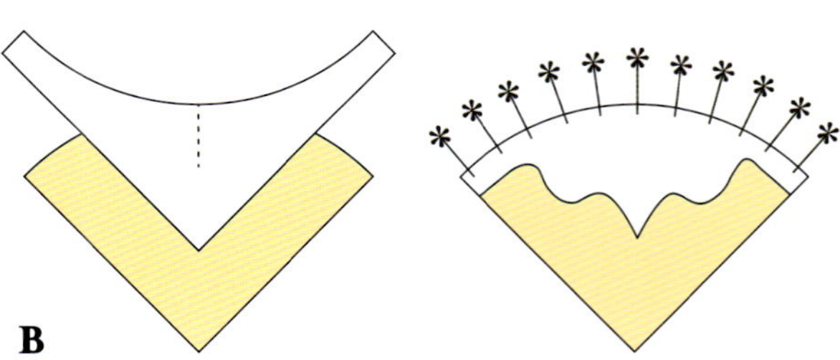
B

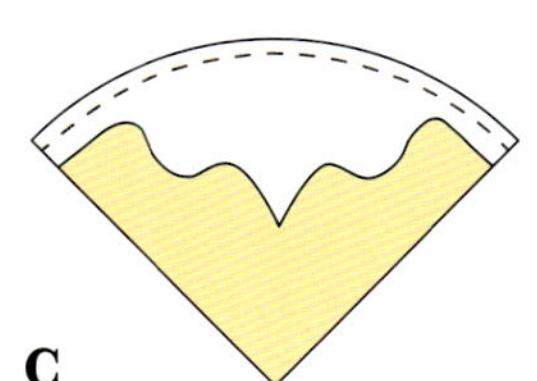
C

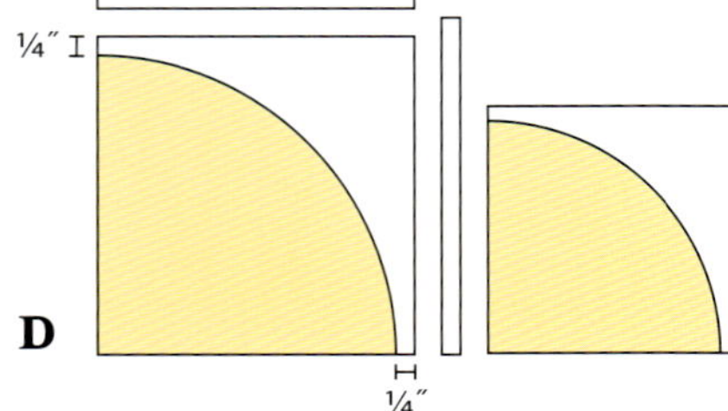

D

5. Repeat Steps 1–4 to make 2 units each of Q2, Q3, and Q4. ***fig. E***

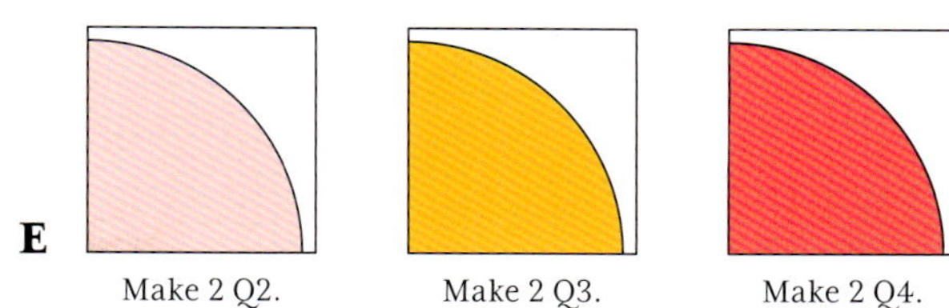

Orange Peel Blocks

1. Pair an A1 piece with a C1 piece. Fold each piece in half to crease the centers. ***fig. F***

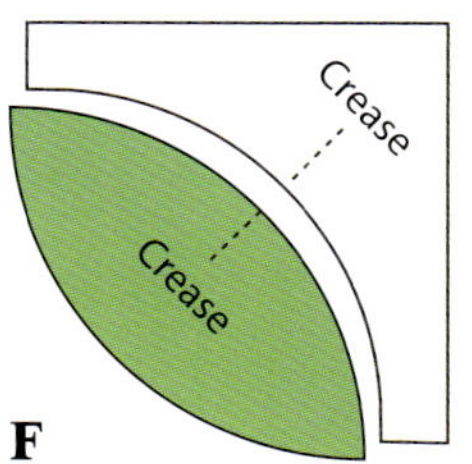

2. Place A1 on C1 RST, lining up the creases. Pin at the center point, then the edges. Pin as often as desired, using more pins if you are new to sewing curves. ***fig. G***

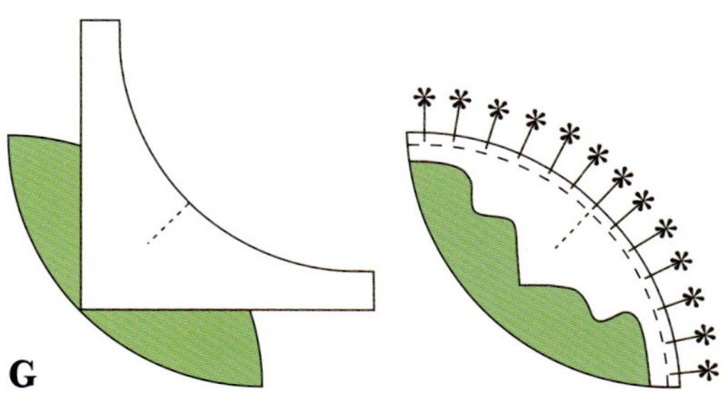

3. Sew with a ¼″ seam along the curve, carefully adjust the fabric as needed. Press the seam toward A1. ***fig. H***

4. Fold an A1 piece in half to crease the center. Place on top of the other edge of the Step 3 C1 piece, RST. Pin the pieces together, ensuring that the A1 piece overlaps the C1 piece by about ¼″ at both ends. Note that the edges will not align perfectly, but you'll have wiggle room for trimming later. ***fig. I***

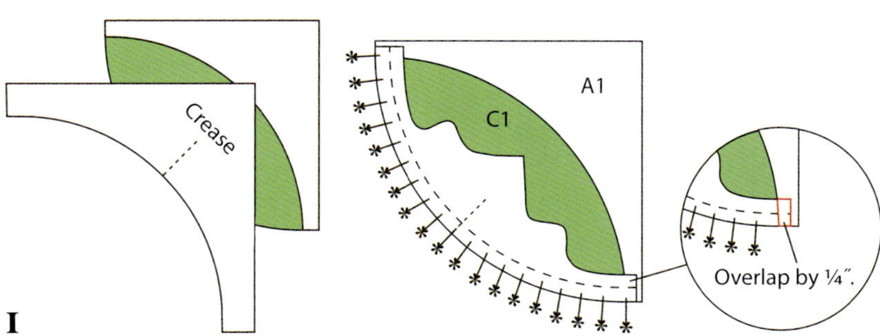

5. Sew with a ¼″ seam allowance. Press the seam toward A. Trim to 7½″ × 7½″. Call this Leaf Unit. ***fig. J***

6. Repeat Steps 1–5 to make a total of 8 Leaf Units. For half of the blocks, press the seams toward A1. For the remaining half, press the seams toward C1. This will ensure that the seams nest when assembling the blocks. ***fig. K***

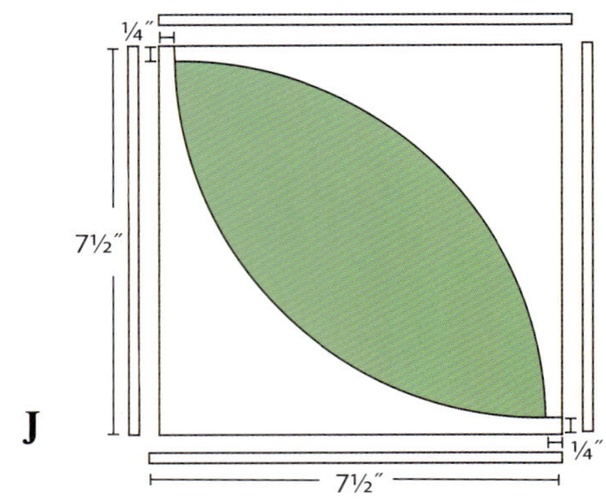

J

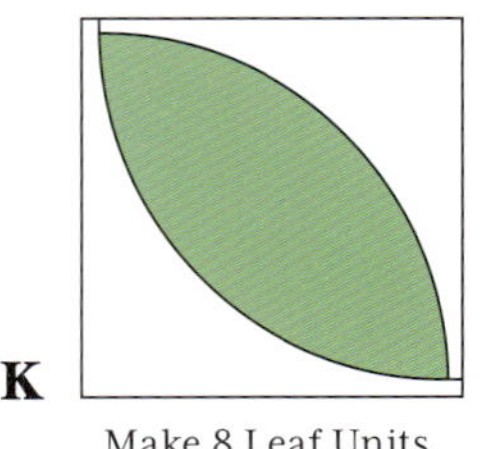
K

Make 8 Leaf Units.

Assemble the Blocks

1. Arrange the following units into 2 rows (***fig. L***):

2. Sew the units into rows, then the rows together. Press the seams open. Each block measures 14½″ × 14½″. Call this Q1 Block. ***fig. M***

3. Repeat Steps 1–2 with Q2, Q3, and Q4 to make the following blocks (***fig. N***):

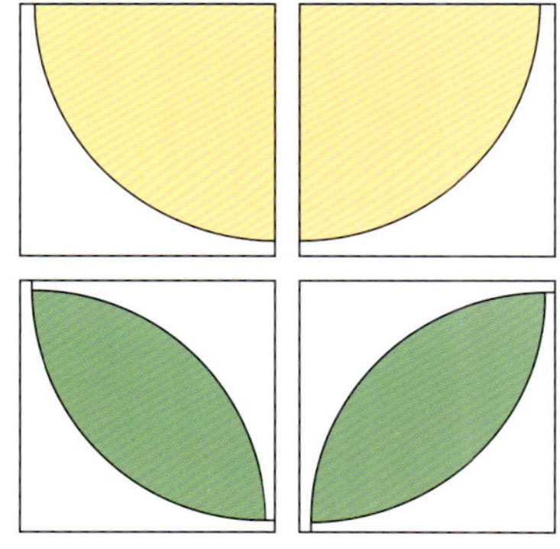
L

Row 1: 2 Q1 Units
Row 2: 2 Leaf Units

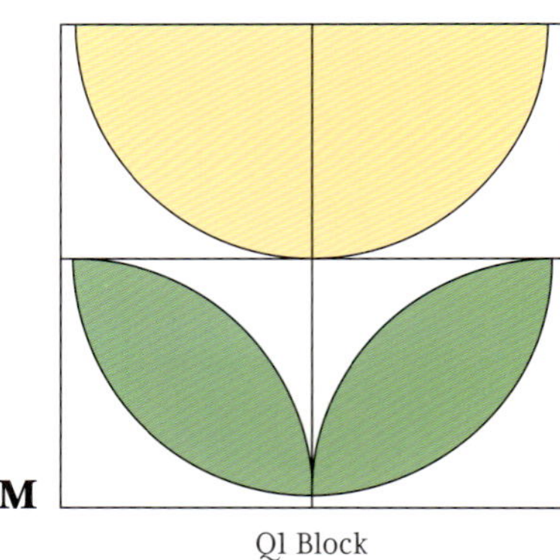
M

Q1 Block

N

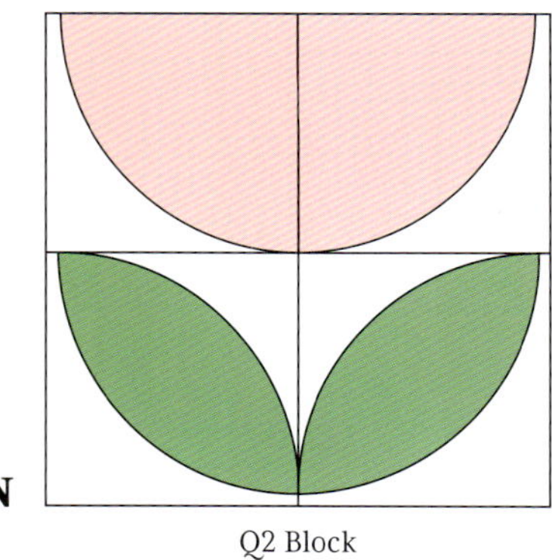
Q2 Block

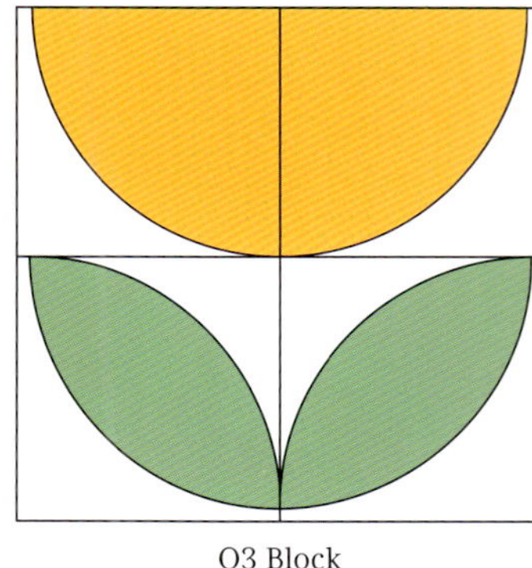
Q3 Block

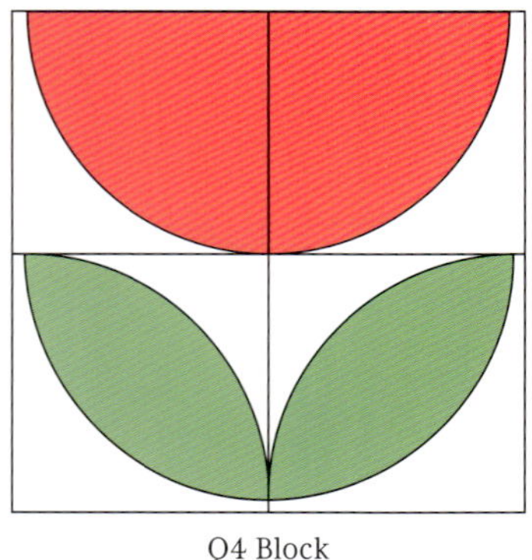
Q4 Block

Assemble the Table Runner

1. Arrange the blocks as follows: A2 strip, Q1 Block, Q2 Block, Q3 Block, Q4 Block, A2 strip. ***fig. O***

2. Sew the units together. Press the seams open.

3. Sew an A3 strip to the top and bottom of the table runner. Press the seams open. The table runner measures 18½″ × 60½″. ***fig. P***

Finish the Quilt

Layer, quilt, and bind the project as desired. See Quilt Assembly (page 24).

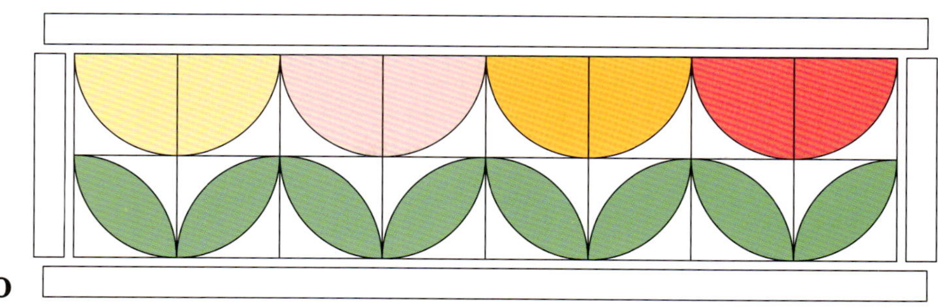

O

P

Reflections Quilt

Flying Geese are the perfect block for the Reflections Quilt, lending themselves beautifully to symmetry and movement. Imagine geese gliding across still water, their reflection mirrored below. It's a calming, timeless image that translates into a quilt design. The no-waste method taught in this chapter is a great choice when you're making lots of geese (and let's be honest, Flying Geese rarely fly solo in a quilt).

FABRIC

Yardages are based on 42″-wide fabric. Fat Quarter (FQ) measures 18″ × 21″. Fat Eighth (F8) measures 9″ × 21″.

Fabric A: 1½ yards

Fabric B: ⅓ yard or 1 FQ

Fabric C: 1⅛ yards

Fabric D: ⅓ yard or 1 FQ

Fabric E: 10″ square or 1 FQ

Fabric F: 10″ square or 1 FQ

Fabric G: ⅓ yard or 1 FQ

Fabric H: ⅛ yard or 1 F8

Fabric J: ½ yard

Binding: ½ yard

Backing: 3½ yards

Batting: 63″ × 63″

Fabric (Solids)

For this quilt, I used Riley Blake Confetti Cottons in Moss, Pewter, Bleached Denim, Curry, Piglet Pink, Riley Aqua, Tangerine, Cement, and Cloud.

Fabric (Prints)

For this quilt, I used Riley Blake Blush 'n Butterscotch in Main Butterscotch, Main Dusty Rose, Dots Cinnamon, Cross Sparkles Dusty Rose, Cross Sparkles Blush, Outlines Blush, Tulips Cream, Confetti Cotton in Salmon and Rose.

Finished Project: 55″ × 55″
Skill Level: Beginner
Pre-Cut Friendly!
Skill Builder: Sewing Flying Geese

CUTTING

FABRIC		
A	B	C
D	E	F
G	H	J

NOTE

The letter "I" has been omitted from the piece letters to avoid any confusion with the number one.

Fabric A (Cloud)

Cut 1 strip 9″ × WOF, subcut into:

- **A1:** 2 squares 9″ × 9″
- **A3:** 4 squares 5″ × 5″

Cut 1 strip 8½″ × WOF, subcut into:

- **A2:** 8 rectangles 8½″ × 4½″

Cut 3 strips 5″ × WOF, subcut into:

- **A3:** 24 squares 5″ × 5″ (total of 28)

Cut 1 strip 4½″ × WOF, subcut into:

- **A4:** 8 squares 4½″ × 4½″

Cut 5 strips 2″ × WOF, sew together and subcut into:

- **A5:** 2 strips 2″ × 45½″
- **A6:** 2 strips 2″ × 48½″

Fabric B (Moss)

Cut 1 strip 9½″ × WOF, subcut into:

- **B1:** 1 square 9½″ × 9½″
- **B2:** 6 squares 5″ × 5″

Fabric C (Pewter)

Cut 1 strip 9½″ × WOF, subcut into:

- **C1:** 1 square 9½″ × 9½″
- **C2:** 8 squares 4½″ × 4½″

Cut 6 strips 4″ × WOF, sewn and subcut into:

- **C3:** 2 strips 4″ × 48½″
- **C4:** 2 strips 4″ × 55½″

Fabric D (Bleached Denim)

D1: 1 square 9½″ × 9½″

D2: 2 squares 5″ × 5″

Fabric E (Curry)

E1: 1 square 9½″ × 9½″

Fabric F (Piglet Pink)

F1: 1 square 9½″ × 9½″

Fabric G (Riley Aqua)

G1: 2 squares 9″ × 9″

Fabric H (Tangerine)

H1: 16 squares 2½″ × 2½″

Fabric J (Cement)

Cut 5 strip 3″ × WOF, sew 3 together and subcut 2 strips into:

- **J2:** 2 strips 3″ × 45½″

Cut remaining strips into:

- **J1:** 2 strips 3″ × 40½″

Binding

Cut 6 strips 2¼″ × width of fabric (WOF).

CONSTRUCTION

Flying Geese Units

1. Follow the steps in How to Sew 4-at-a-Time No-Waste Flying Geese (right) to make 4 A3B1 Flying Geese. Trim to 4½″ × 8½″. ***fig. A***

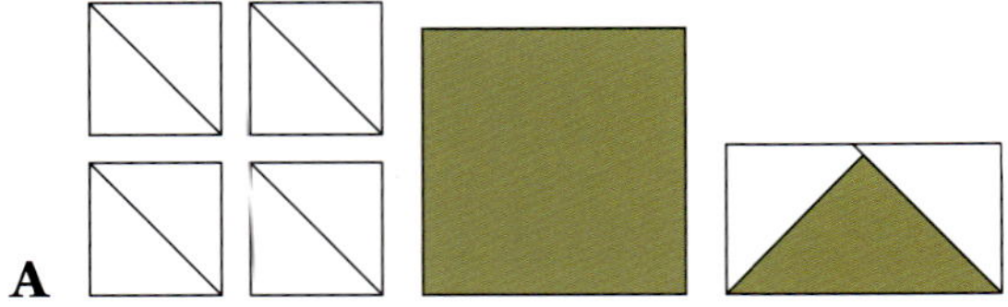

A

2. Follow the steps in How to Sew 4-at-a-Time No-Waste Flying Geese (right) to make the following units (***fig. B***):

   Make 4 A3C1, 4 A3D1, 4 A3E1, and 4 A3F1 Flying Geese units. Set aside 2 A3F1 Flying Geese for a future project.

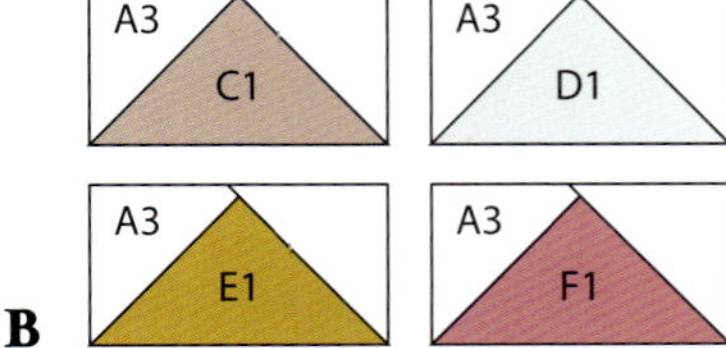

B

How to Sew 4-At-a-Time No-Waste Flying Geese

If you want to sew 4-at-a-time Flying Geese of different sizes, use these formulas:

Large square size + 1½″ = finished width of Flying Geese

Small square size + 1″ = finished height of Flying Geese

1. Pair 4 small squares (5″ × 5″) with a larger square (9½″ × 9½″). Draw a diagonal line on the wrong side of all of the smaller squares. ***fig. A***

2. Place 2 small squares on opposite corners of the large square RST, with the drawn lines along the large square's diagonal. Sew ¼″ away from both sides of the drawn lines. Cut on the drawn line, and press the seams open. ***fig. B***

3. Layer the remaining 2 small squares on the corners of the Step 2 units, correctly orienting the drawn lines. Sew ¼″ away from both sides of the drawn line. Cut on the drawn line, and press the seams open to complete 4 Flying Geese. ***fig. C***

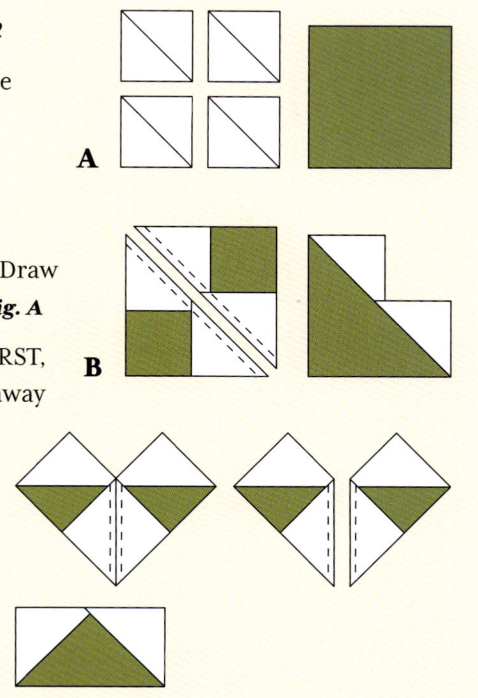

Snowball Corner Units

1. Draw a diagonal line on the wrong side of all 16 H1 squares.

2. Place an H1 square on the top right corner of an A2 rectangle RST. Sew on the drawn line. ***fig. C***

3. Trim off the corner ¼″ away from the seam. Press the seam open. Call this Unit A2H1-Right. Repeat Step 2 to make 4 units. ***fig. D***

4. Repeat Steps 2–3, placing the H1 square on the top left corner of an A2 rectangle RST, to make 4 units. ***fig. E***

5. Repeat Steps 2–3, placing the H1 square on a corner of an A4 square RST, to make 8 units. ***fig. F***

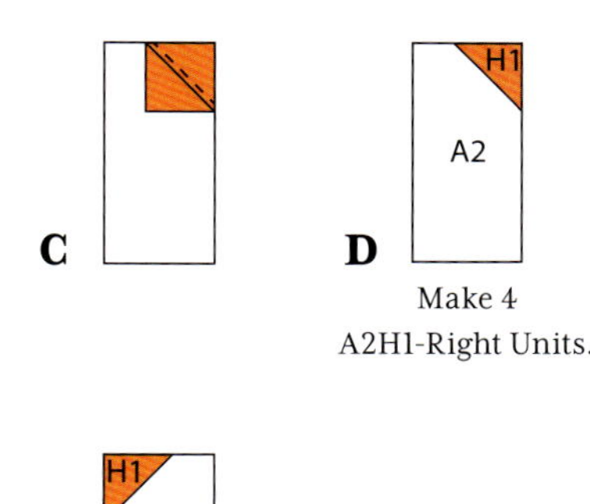

Make 4 A2H1-Right Units.

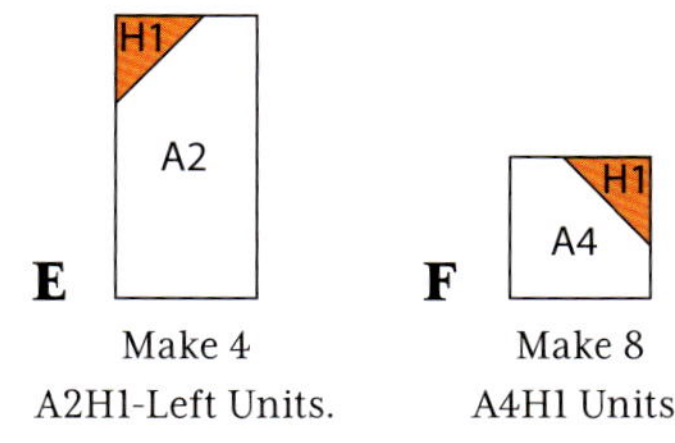

Make 4 A2H1-Left Units.

Make 8 A4H1 Units.

Half-Square Triangle Units (HST)

1. Follow the instructions in How to Make 2-at-a-Time HSTS (page 36) to make 12 A3B2 HSTs, 4 A3D2 HSTs. Trim to 8½″ × 8½″.

2. Follow the instructions in How to Make 2-at-a-Time HSTS (page 36) to make 4 A1G1 HSTs. Trim to 8½″ × 8½″. ***fig. G***

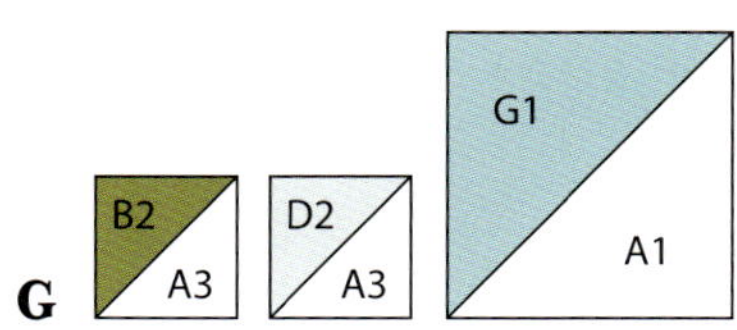

Corner Units

1. Arrange the following units into 3 rows (***fig. H***):

   Row 1: A1G1 HST, Unit A2H1-Right, Unit A4H1, A3B2 HST

   Row 2: Unit A2H1-Left, A3B2 HST, C2 square

   Row 3: Unit A4H1, A3B2 HST, C2 square, A3D2 HST

2. Sew the units into rows, then sew the rows together. Press the seams open. Call this Corner Unit, measuring 16½″ × 16½″. Repeat to make a total of 4 Corner Units. ***fig. I***

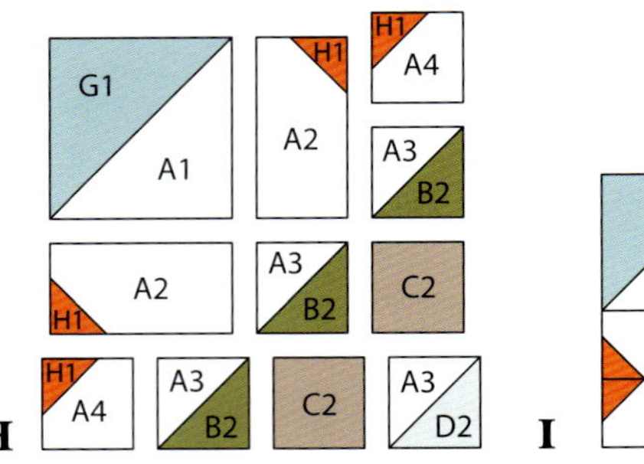

Units FG1 and FG2

1. Arrange and sew an A3B1, an A3C1, an A3D1, and an A3E1 Flying Geese together into a vertical column. Press the seams open. Call this Unit FG1. Repeat to make a second Unit FG1. ***fig. J***

2. Arrange and sew an A3B1, an A3C1, an A3D1, an A3E1, and an A3F1 Flying Geese together into a vertical column as shown. Press the seams open. Call this Unit FG2. Repeat to make a second Unit FG2. ***fig. K***

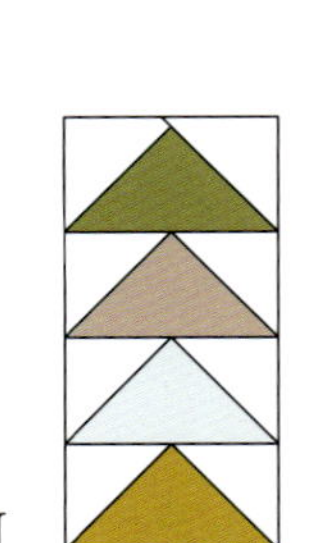

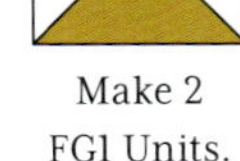
Make 2 FG1 Units.

Make 2 FG2 Units.

Assemble the Quilt

1. Arrange the following units into 3 rows (***fig. L***):

   Row 1: Corner Unit, FG1 Unit, Corner Unit

   Row 2: 2 FG2 Units

   Row 3: Corner Unit, FG1 Unit, Corner Unit

2. Sew the units into rows, then the rows together. Press seams open. ***fig. M***

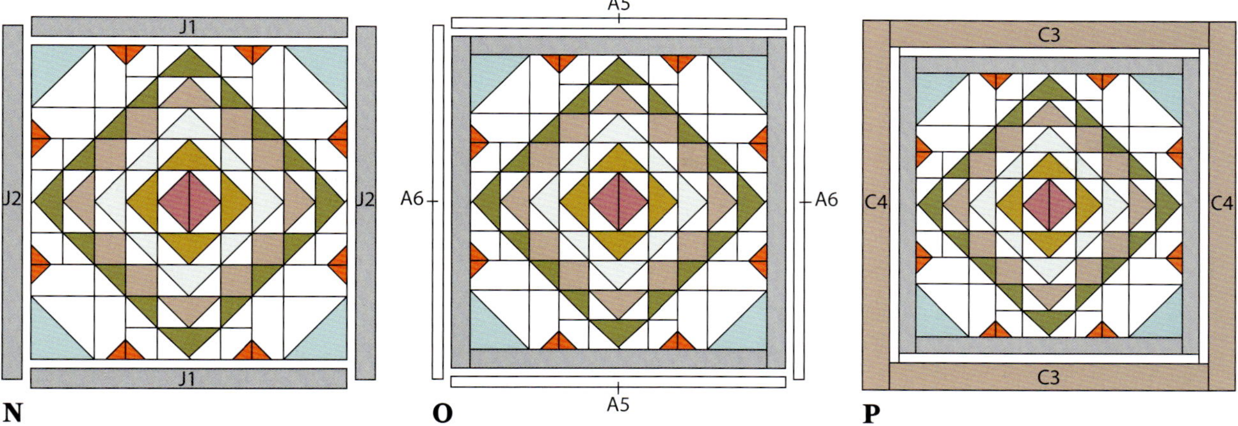

3. Sew J1 border strips to the top and bottom of the unit. Press the seams toward the strips. Sew J2 border strips to both sides of the unit. Press the seams toward the strips. ***fig. N***

4. Sew A5 border strips to the top and bottom of the unit. Press the seams toward the strips. Sew 2 A6 border strips to both sides of the unit. Press the seams toward the strips. ***fig. O***

5. Sew C3 border strips to the top and bottom of the unit. Press the seams toward the strips. Sew C4 border strips to both sides of the unit. Press the seams toward the strips. ***fig. P***

Finish the Quilt

Layer, quilt, and bind the project as desired. See Quilt Assembly (page 24).

MINI PROJECT

Modern Migration Wall Hanging

This Flying Geese wall hanging is a classic quilting project that combines tradition with a touch of modern flair. It's a fun way to dive into piecing and add a bold, eye-catching touch to your space. For more on Flying Geese, see Reflections (page 62).

MATERIALS

Yardages are based on 42″-wide fabric. Fat Quarter (FQ) measures 18″ × 21″.

Fabric A (Dark Yellow): 1 FQ

Fabric B (Light Yellow): 1 FQ

Fabric C (White): 1 FQ

Binding: ¼ yard

Backing: ¾ yard

Batting: 25″ × 28″

Fabric

For the solids wall hanging, I used Riley Blake Sparkler in Vintage White, Beehive, and Daisy. The print wall hanging uses scraps from my stash.

Finished Project: 17″ × 20″
Skill Level: Beginner
Pre-Cut Friendly!
Skill Builder: Sewing Flying Geese

CUTTING

Fabric A (Daisy)

Cut 1 strip 5½″ × 21″; subcut into:

- **A1:** 2 rectangles 5½″ × 4″
- **A2:** 2 rectangles 5½″ × 1½″

Cut 2 strips 3½″ × 21″; subcut into:

- **A3:** 12 squares 3½″ × 3½″

Fabric B (Beehive)

Cut 1 strip 5½″ × 21″; subcut into:

- **B1:** 2 rectangles 5½″ × 4″
- **B2:** 2 rectangles 5½″ × 1½″

Cut 2 strips 3½″ × 21″; subcut into:

- **B3:** 12 squares 3½″ × 3½″

Fabric C (Vintage White)

Cut 2 strips 6½″ × 21″; subcut into:

- **C1:** 6 squares 6½″ × 6½″

Binding

Cut into 3 strips 2¼″ × width of fabric (WOF).

CONSTRUCTION

Flying Geese Units

1. Follow the instructions in How to Sew 4-at-a-Time No-Waste Flying Geese (page 65) to make a total of 12 A3 and C1 Flying Geese. Trim to 3″ × 5½″. Set aside 2 units for a future project. ***fig. A***

2. Repeat Step 1 to make 12 B3 and C1 Flying Geese. Trim to 3″ × 5½″. Set aside 2 units for a future project. ***fig. B***

Unit A1 and A2

1. Sew 3 AC Flying Geese together in a vertical column. Sew an A2 rectangle to the top of the AC Flying Geese unit. Press the seams open. Call this Unit A1. Repeat to make a second Unit A1. ***fig. C***

2. Sew 3 BC Flying Geese together in a vertical column. Sew a Fabric B2 rectangle to the bottom of the BC Flying Geese unit. Press the seams open. Call this Unit A2. Repeat to make a second Unit A2. ***fig. D***

A

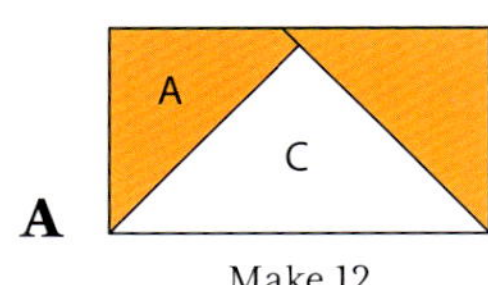

Make 12
AC Flying Geese.

B

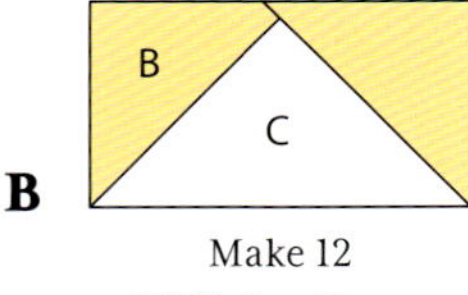

Make 12
BC Flying Geese.

C

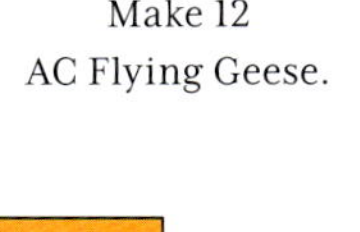

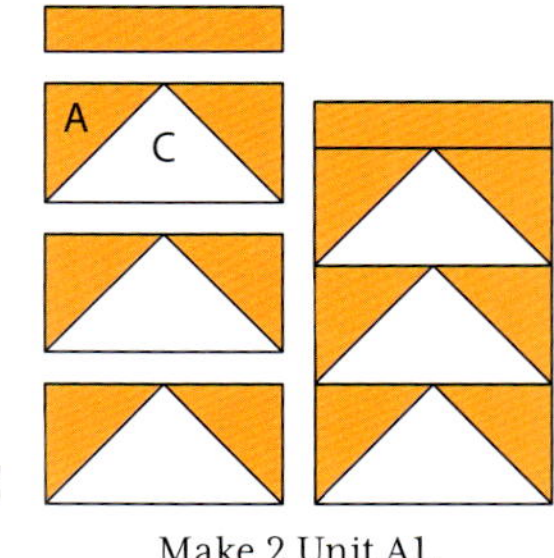

Make 2 Unit A1.

D

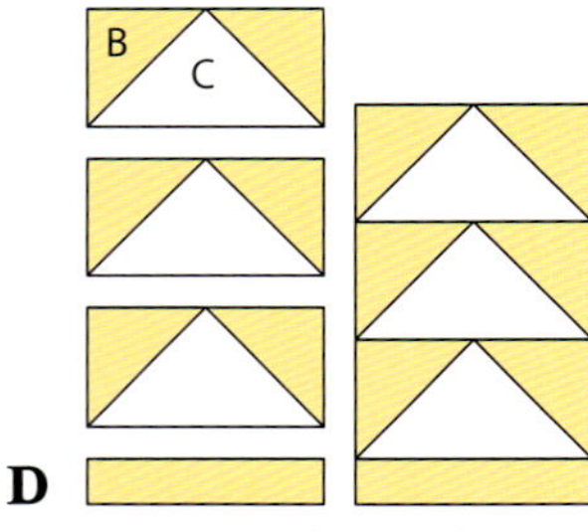

Make 2 Unit A2.

Unit B1 and B2

1. Sew 2 AC Flying Geese together in a vertical pair. Press the seam open. Sew an A1 rectangle to the right side of the AC Flying Geese unit. Press the seam toward the A1 rectangle. Call this Unit B1. Repeat to make a second Unit B1. ***fig. E***

2. Sew 2 BC Flying Geese together in a vertical pair. Press the seam open. Sew a B1 rectangle to the right side of the BC Flying Geese unit. Press the seam toward the B1 rectangle. Call this Unit B2. Repeat to make a second Unit B2. ***fig. F***

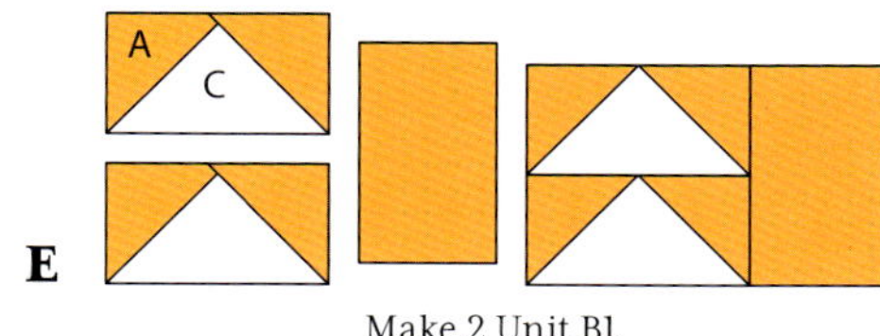

Make 2 Unit B1.

Make 2 Unit B2.

Assemble the Quilt

1. Arrange the units into 4 rows as shown. ***fig. G***

   Row 1: Unit B1, Unit A2

   Row 2: Unit B2, Unit A1

   Row 3: Unit A1, Unit B2

   Row 4: Unit A2, Unit B1

2. Sew the units into rows. Press the seams of Row 1 and Row 3 to the right. Press the seams of Row 2 and Row 4 to the left.

3. Sew the rows together, nesting the seams. Press the seams open. ***fig. H***

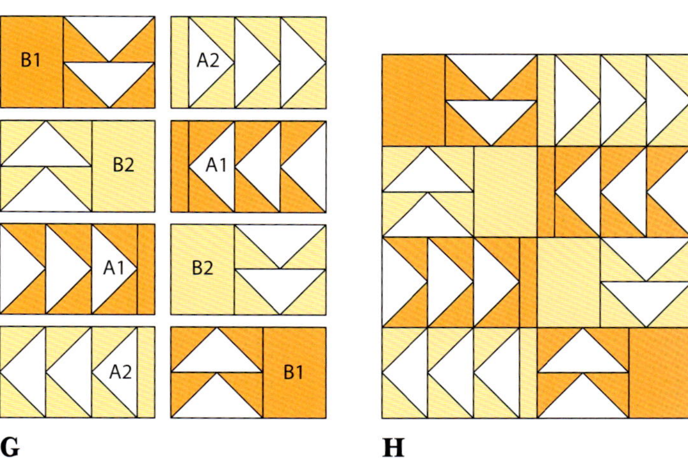

Finish the Quilt

Layer, quilt, and bind the project as desired. See Quilt Assembly (page 24).

Candyland Quilt

The Candyland Quilt is a playful design that adds a touch of joy and color to your quilting practice. This quilt uses strip-piecing, where long strips of fabric are sewn together before cutting them into smaller pieces for the quilt block. It's a great way to speed up the process while maintaining precision when working with patterns that require repeating elements.

You can also get creative by adding your favorite fussy cut fabric to the negative space (A2 square in the cutting list), or even turn it into a memory quilt by using t-shirts to fill the space. Make this Candyland Quilt uniquely yours!

Strip Piecing

Here are some tips for strip-piecing:

- Pre-press the fabric before cutting strips to remove wrinkles or creases.
- A consistent ¼˝ seam allowance helps keep everything aligned and prevents distortion.
- Don't pull the fabric. Gently feed the strips through the machine to avoid stretching.
- Press after each seam before adding the next strips to prevent distortion.
- Alternate the starting point when sewing strips together. Sew the first strip from one end to the other, then reverse the direction by starting where you just finished. This distributes the tension more evenly across the fabric.

MATERIALS

Yardages are based on 42˝-wide fabric.

Fabric A: 2⅞ yards

Fabric B: ½ yard

Fabric C: ¼ yard

Fabric D: ½ yard

Fabric E: ¼ yard

Fabric F: ¼ yard

Fabric G: ¼ yard

Fabric H: ¼ yard

Binding: ½ yard

Backing: 4 yards

Batting: 72˝ × 72˝

Fabric

In this quilt, I used Riley Blake Confetti Cotton in Pink Dogwood, Boy Blue, Petunia, Riley Mustard, Salmon, Seafoam, Jazzberry, and Dainty Daisy in Cloud White.

Finished Project: 64″ × 64″
Skill Level: Beginner
Skill Builder: Strip Piecing

CUTTING

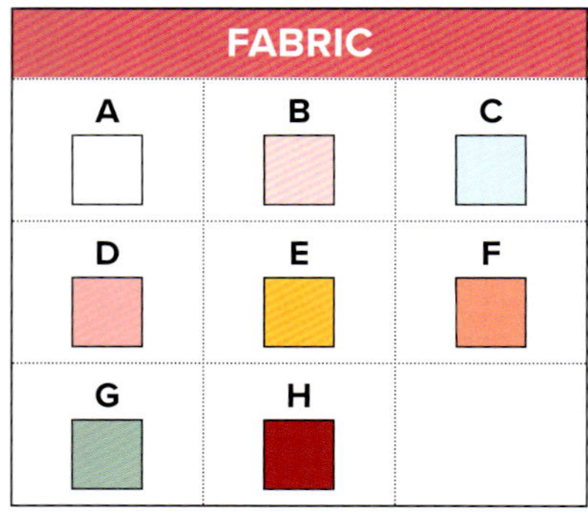

Fabric A (Dainty Daisy in Cloud White)

Cut 1 strip 16½″ × WOF, subcut into:

- **A1:** 16 strips 2½″ × 16½″

Cut 3 strips 12½″ × WOF, subcut into:

- **A2:** 8 squares 12½″ × 12½″
- **A5:** 8 strips 2½″ × 12½″

Cut 3 strips 4½″ × WOF, subcut into:

- **A3:** 3 strips 4½″ × WOF

Cut 11 strips 2½″ × WOF, subcut into:

- **A4:** 8 strips 2½″ × WOF
- **A5:** 8 strips 2½″ × 12½″ (total of 16)

Fabric B (Pink Dogwood)

B1: Cut 1 strip 4½″ × WOF

B2: Cut 2 strips 2½″ × WOF

Fabric C (Boy Blue)

C1: Cut 2 strips 2½″ × WOF

Fabric D (Petunia)

D1: Cut 1 strip 4½″ × WOF

D2: Cut 2 strips 2½″ × WOF

Fabric E (Mustard)

E1: Cut 2 strips 2½″ × WOF

Fabric F (Salmon)

F1: Cut 2 strips 2½″ × WOF

Fabric G (Seafoam)

G1: Cut 2 strips 2½″ × WOF

Fabric H (Jazzberry)

H1: Cut 2 strips 2½″ × WOF

Binding

Cut 7 strips 2¼″ × width of fabric (WOF).

CONSTRUCTION

Seam allowances are ¼″ unless otherwise noted.

Make Strip Sets

1. Arrange 2 A3 strips and a B1 strip into 3 rows. Sew together, and press all seams in one direction, toward the A3 strip. ***fig. A***

2. Cut the Step 1 unit into 16 strips 2½″ × 12½″. Call this Strip Set 1 (SS1). ***fig. B***

3. Arrange 2 A4 strips, 2 C1 strips, and a D1 strip into 5 rows. Sew together, and press all seams in one direction. ***fig. C***

4. Cut the Step 3 units into 16 strips 2½″ × 12½″. Call this Strip Set 2 (SS2). ***fig. D***

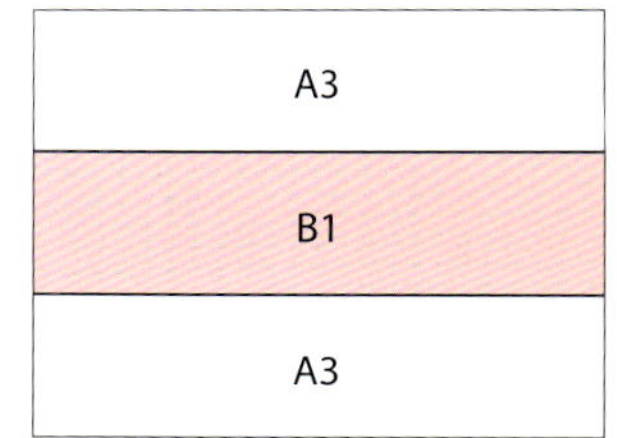

A

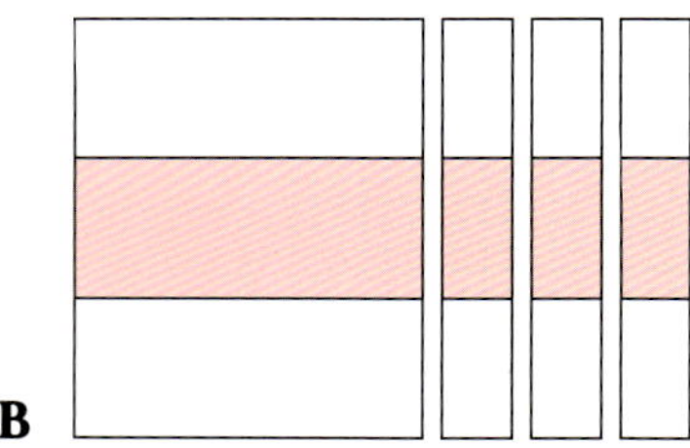

B

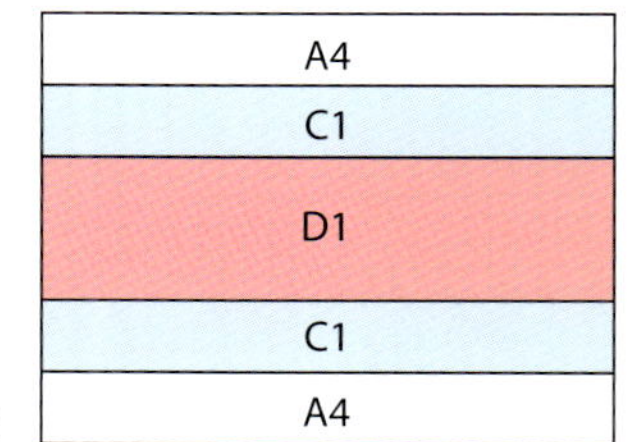

C

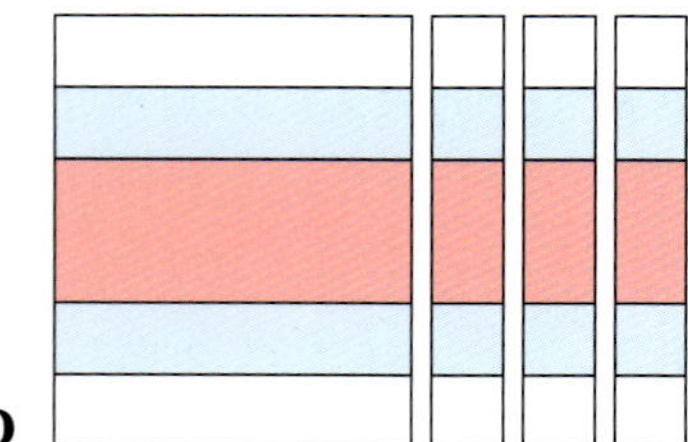

D

5. Arrange 2 B2 strips, 2 D2 strips, and an A3 strip into 5 rows. Sew together, and press all the seams in one direction. ***fig. E***

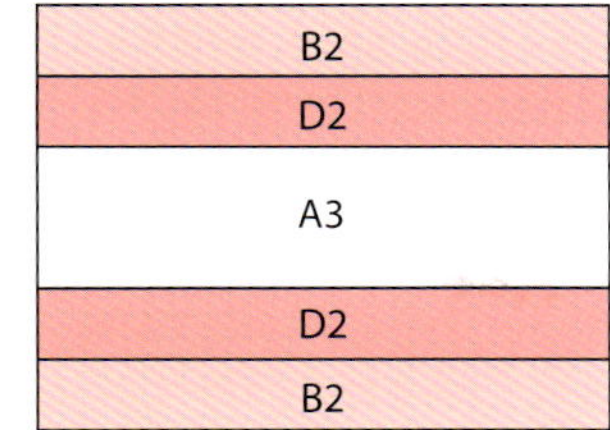

E

6. Cut the Step 5 unit into 8 strips 4½˝ × 12½˝. Call this Strip Set 3 (SS3). ***fig. F***

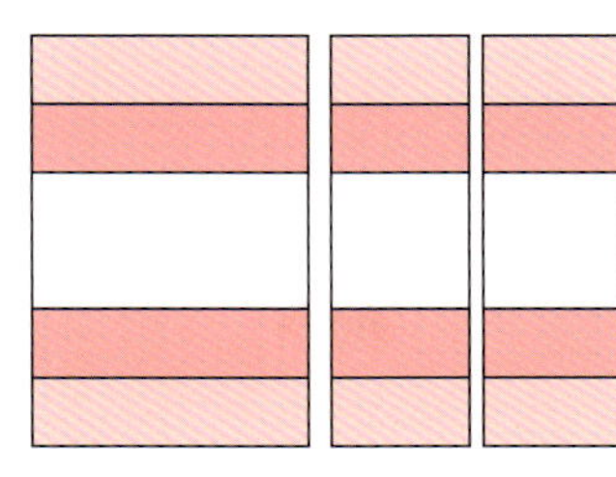

F

7. Arrange an E1 strip, 2 A4 strips, a F1 strip, a G1 strip, and an H1 strip into 6 rows. Sew together, and press all the seams in one direction, toward the E1 strip. ***fig. G***

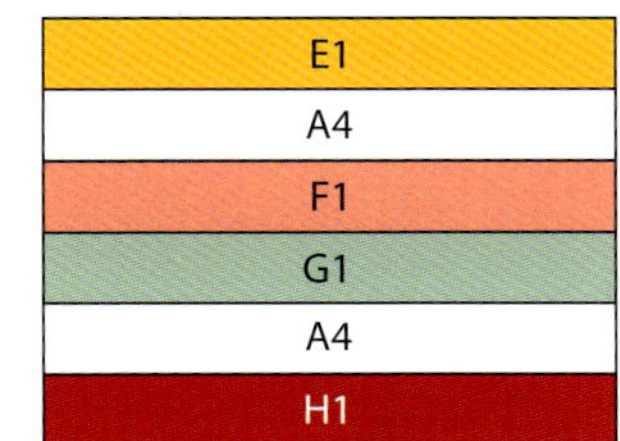

G

8. Cut the Step 7 unit into 16 strips 2½˝ × 12½˝. Call this Strip Set 4 (SS4) ***fig. H***

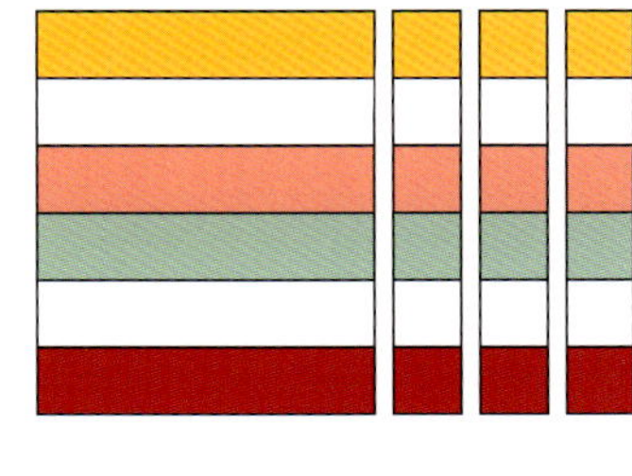

H

9. Arrange 4 A4 strips, an E1 strip, a F1 strip, a G1 strip, and an H1 strip into 8 rows. Sew together, and press the seams in one direction. ***fig. I***

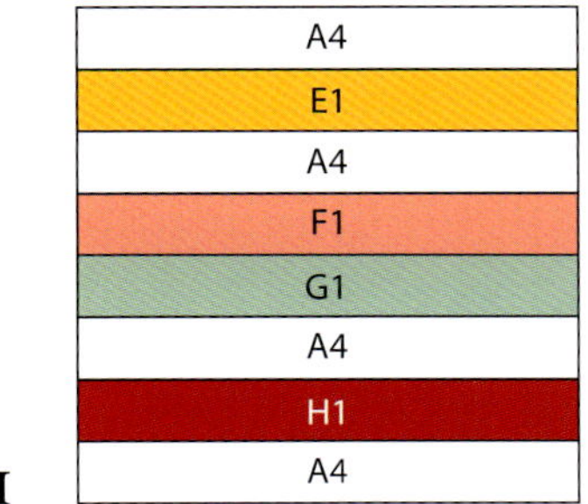

I

10. Cut the Step 9 unit into 16 strips 2½˝ × 16½˝. Call this Strip Set 5 (SS5). ***fig. J***

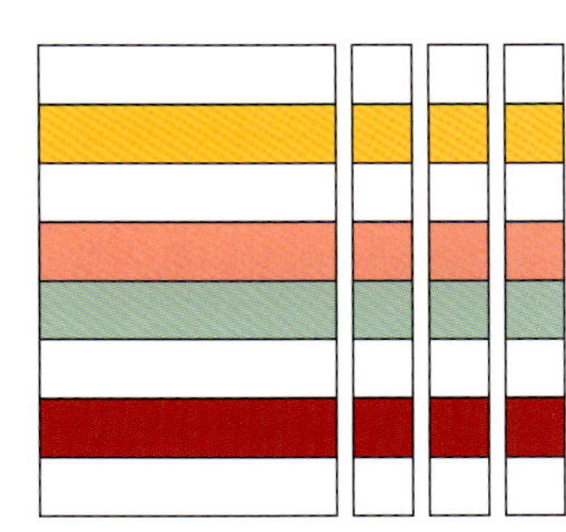

J

Make Block A

1. Arrange the following units into 5 rows as shown. ***fig. K***

K

2. Rotate the strips as needed to nest the seams and sew the rows together. Press the seams open.

3. Sew A5 strips to both sides of the units. Press the seams toward the A5 strips. ***fig. L***

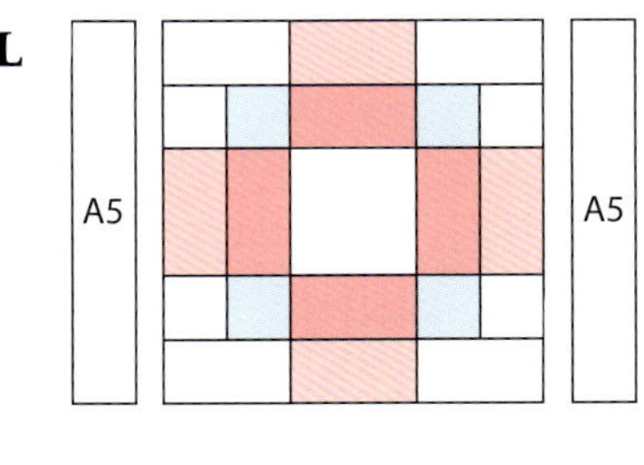

L

4. Sew A1 strips to the top and bottom of the unit. Press the seams toward the A1 strips to complete Block A (16½˝ × 16½˝). ***fig. M***

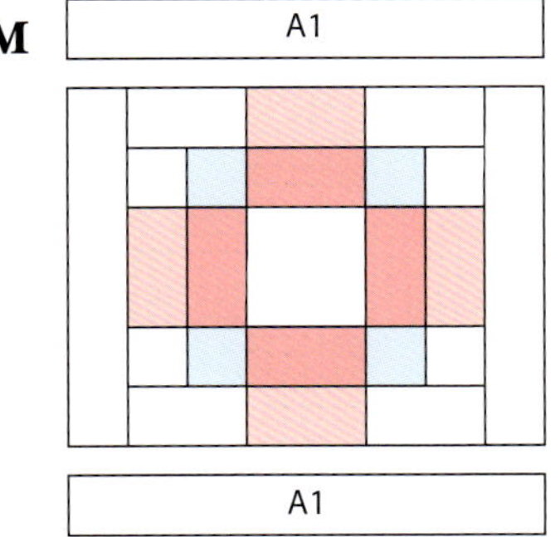

M

5. Repeat Steps 1–4 to make a total of 8 Block As. ***fig. N***

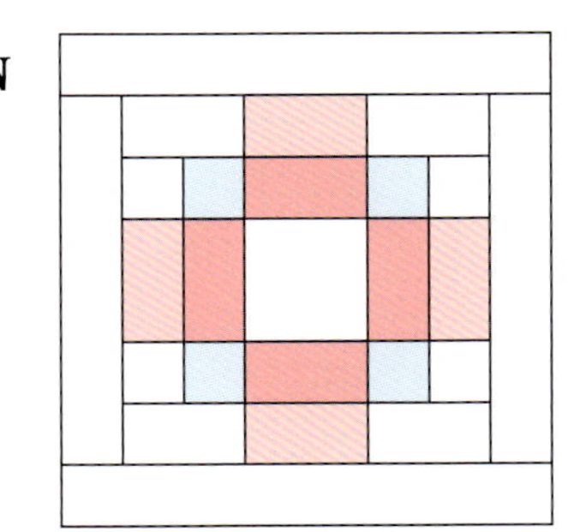

N

Make Block B

1. Arrange the following units into 3 rows ***(fig. O)***:

   Row 1: SS4

   Row 2: A2 square

   Row 3: SS4

2. Sew the rows together, and press the seams away from the A2 square.

3. Sew SS5 strips to both sides of the unit. Press the seams open, completing Block B (16½″ × 16½″). ***fig. P***

4. Repeat Steps 1–3 to make a total of 8 Block Bs. ***fig. Q***

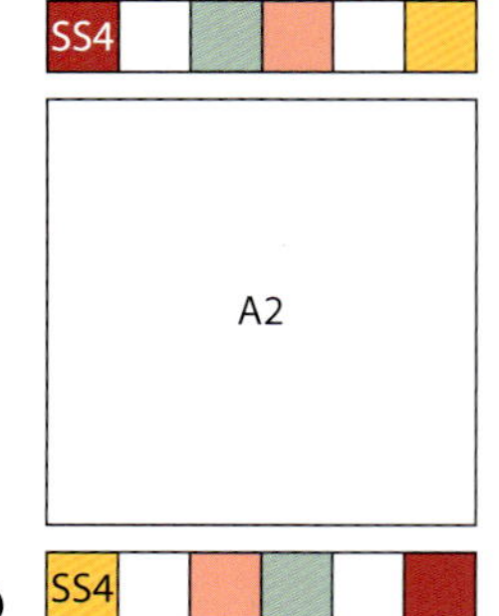

O

P

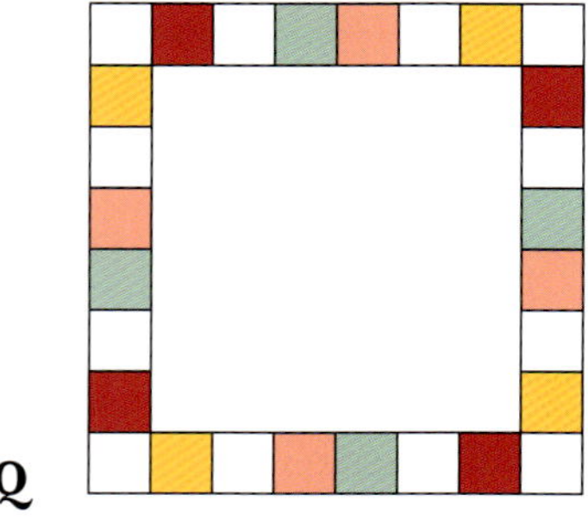

Q

Assemble the Quilt

1. Arrange the following units into 4 rows: ***fig. R***

   Row 1: Block B, Block A, Block B, Block A

   Row 2: Block A, Block B, Block A, Block B

   Row 3: Block B, Block A, Block B, Block A

   Row 4: Block A, Block B, Block A, Block B

2. Sew the units into rows. Press the seams toward the Block Bs. Sew the rows together. Press the seams open. The quilt top measures 64½″ × 64½″. ***fig. S***

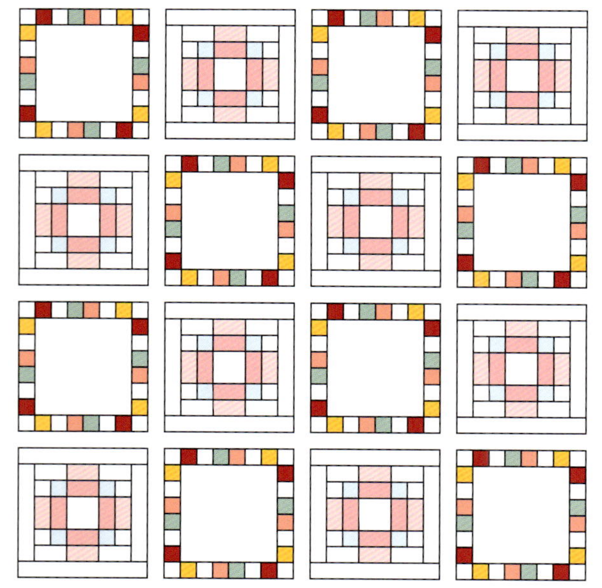

R

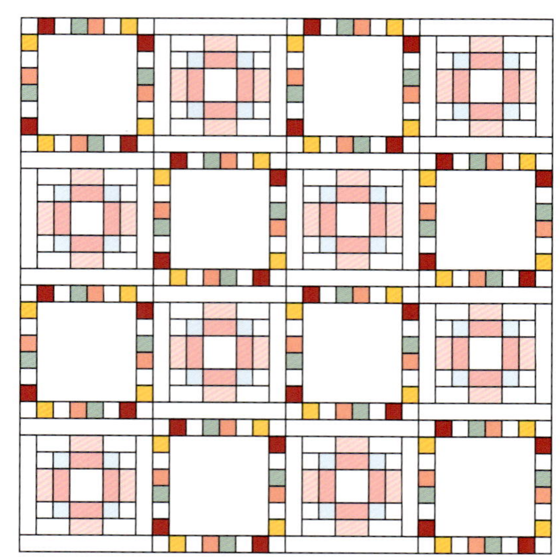

S

Finish the Quilt

Layer, quilt, and bind the project as desired. See Quilt Assembly (page 24).

Windmill Quilt

The Windmill quilt focuses on mastering the Square-in-a-Square block. As the name suggests, this block features a square in the center, surrounded by four right angled-triangles. Sewing with right angled-triangles means working with bias edges.

Working on this bias means working with fabric cut on the diagonal, at a 45-degree angle to the selvage. Bias cut shapes are more prone to stretching out of shape if not handled carefully.

Sewing Square-in-a-Square Blocks

Here are some helpful tips for making a Square-in-a-Square block:

- Use starch to help stabilize bias edges and prevent them from stretching.
- Pin to keep the pieces from shifting or being pulled.
- Pressing matters. Lift the iron off the fabric, and then set it back down on the seam or section instead of sliding the iron back and forth.

MATERIALS

Yardages are based on 42˝-wide fabric. Fat Eighth (F8) measures 9˝ × 21˝. Backing Fabric requirement is calculated for non-directional fabric.

Fabric A: 2⅝ yards

Accent Fabrics: 12 F8s

Binding: ½ yard

Backing: 3⅓ yards

Batting: 59˝ × 76˝

Fabric

For this quilt, I used Riley Blake Blossom in Honey, Pumpkin, Orange, Peony, Wisteria, Eggplant, Aqua, Peacock, Denim, Tone-on-Tone White, Dainty Daisy in Grass, Holly, and Jade.

Finished Project: 51˝ × 68˝
Skill Level: Advanced Beginner
Pre-Cut Friendly!
Skill Builder: Sewing Square-in-a-Square Blocks

CUTTING

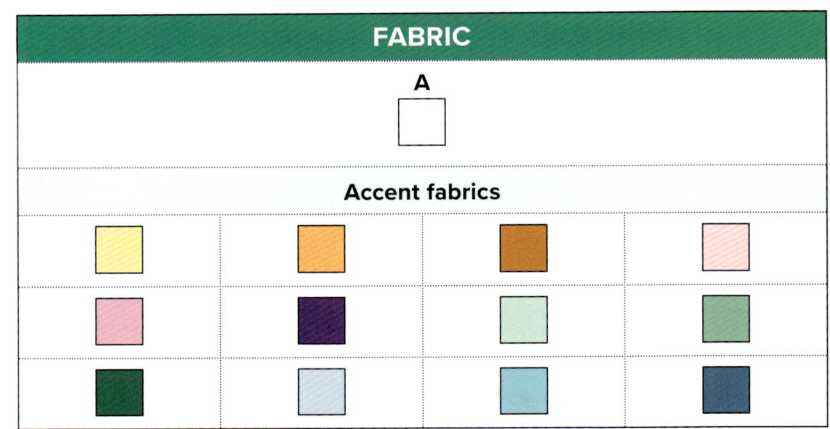

Fabric A (Blossom Tone-on-Tone White)

Cut 6 strips 9½″ × WOF, subcut into:

- **A1:** 24 squares 9½″ × 9½″

Cut 8 strips 3½″ × WOF, subcut into:

- **A2:** 96 squares 3½″ × 3½″

Cut 1 strip 2½″ × WOF, subcut into:

- **A3:** 12 squares 2½″ × 2½″

Accent Fabrics

From each of 12 F8s, cut:

- **B1:** 4 squares 4⅛″ × 4⅛″
- **B2:** 4 rectangles 2½″ × 5½″

Binding

Cut into 7 strips 2¼″ × width of fabric (WOF).

CONSTRUCTION

Seam allowances are ¼″ unless otherwise noted.

Square-in-a-Square Blocks

1. Cut all A1 and A2 squares diagonally. You will have 48 A1 triangles and 192 A2 triangles. ***fig. A***

2. Fold all of the triangles from Step 1 in half, creasing the center of the long side. Set all A1 triangles aside for Windmill Blocks.

3. Fold a B1 square in half to form a crease. Fold in half again the other way to create a perpendicular crease.

4. Arrange 2 A2 triangles on opposite sides of a B1 square, aligning the creases. ***fig. B***

5. Sew the triangles to the B1 square RST. Press the seams toward the A2 triangles, and trim the dog ears. ***fig. C***

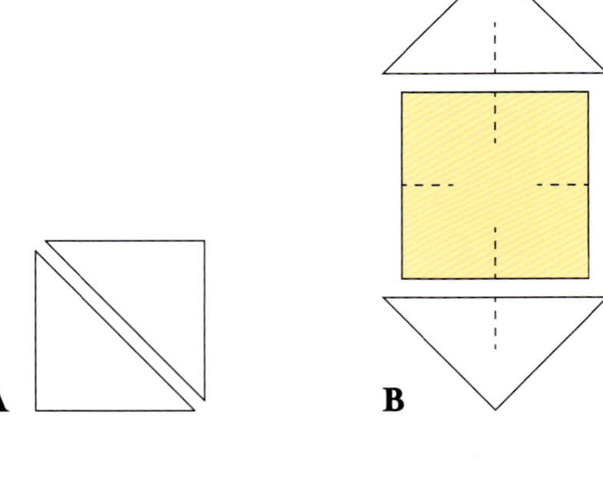

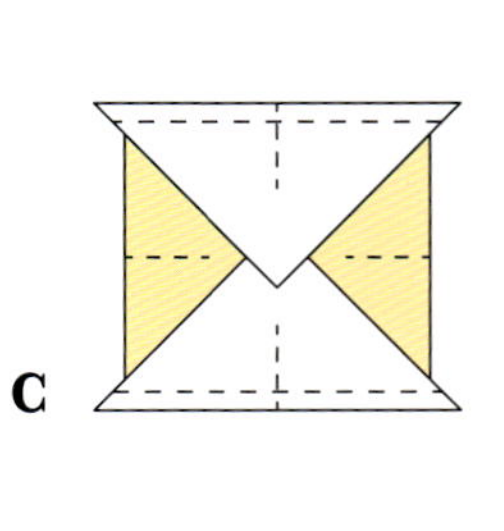

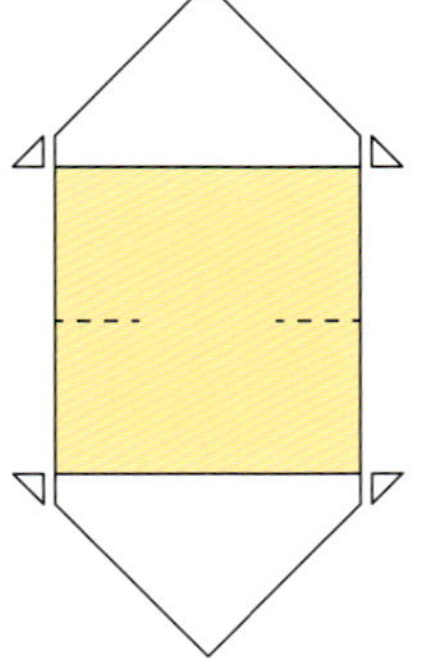

6. Sew 2 A2 triangles to the remaining sides of the B1 square RST. Press the seams toward A1 square. Trim to 5½″ × 5½″. Make sure to leave a ¼″ seam allowance beyond each corner of the B1 square as you trim. Call this Unit SQ1. ***fig. D***

7. Repeat Steps 2–6 with 3 remaining B2 squares from the same colorway to make a total of 4 Units SQ1.

8. Gather the 44 remaining B1 squares and 176 remaining A2 triangles. Use the same method as Steps 2–7 to make 4 SQ units from each colorway. ***fig. E***

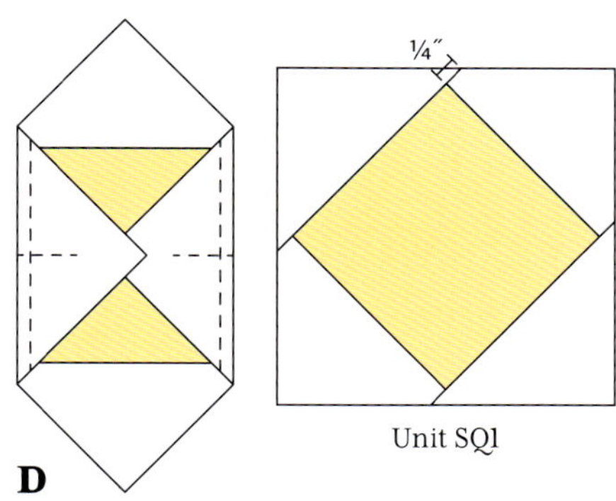

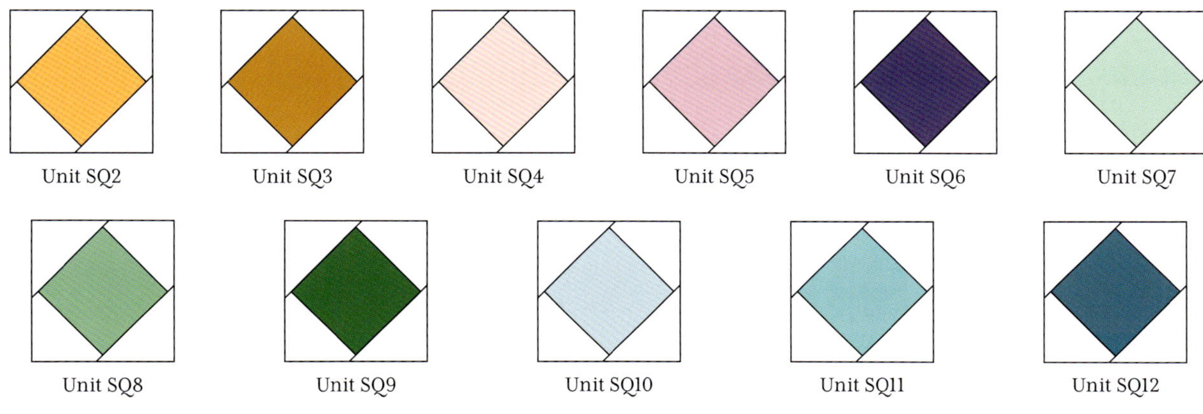

E

Windmill Blocks

1. Arrange the following units into 3 rows (***fig. F***):

   Row 1: Unit SQ, B2 rectangle, Unit SQ

   Row 2: B2 rectangle, A3 square, B2 rectangle

   Row 3: Unit SQ, B2 rectangle, Unit SQ

2. Sew the units into rows. Press the seams toward the B2 rectangles.

3. Sew the rows together and press the seams toward Row 2. The Windmill Block measures 12½″ × 12½″. ***fig. G***

4. Fold the Windmill Block in half to form a crease. Fold in half again to create a second crease perpendicular to the first.

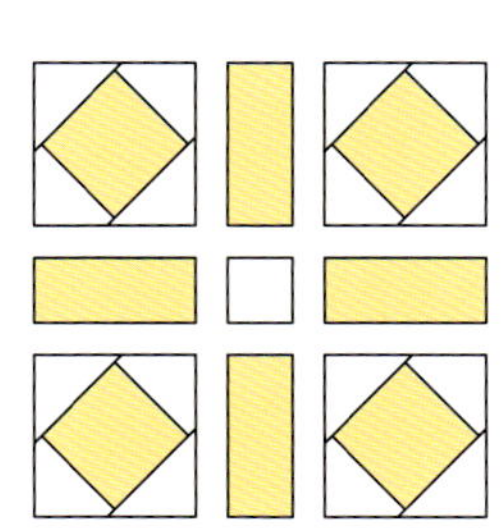

F

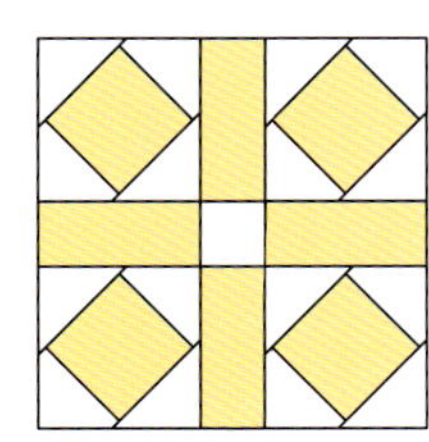

G

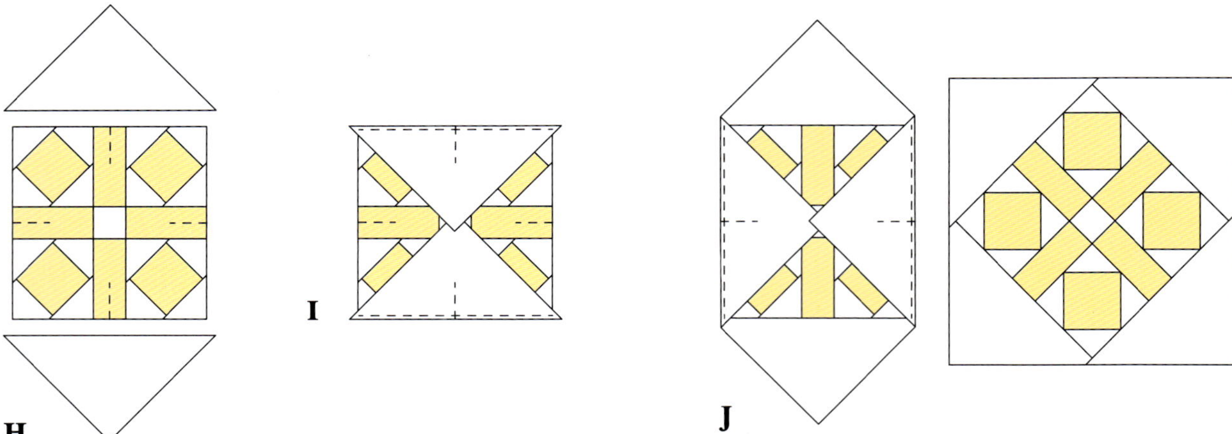

5. Arrange 2 A1 triangles on opposite sides of the Windmill Block, aligning the creases. ***fig. H***

6. Sew the A1 triangles to the Windmill Block RST. Press the seams open. ***fig. I***

7. Arrange and sew 2 Fabric A1 triangles to the remaining sides of the block RST. Press the seams open. Trim to 17½″ × 17½″. ***fig. J***

8. Repeat Steps 1–7 with the remaining sets of SQ units, B2 rectangles, and A3 squares to make a total of 12 blocks.

Assemble the Quilt

1. Arrange the units into 4 rows of 3 Windmill Blocks as shown.

2. Sew the units into rows. Follow the arrows for pressing direction. ***fig. K***

3. Nest the seams as you sew the rows together. Press the seams open. The quilt top measures 51½″ × 68½″. ***fig. L***

Finish the Quilt

Layer, quilt, and bind the project as desired. See Quilt Assembly (page 24).

Entwined Quilt

The quarter-square triangle (QST) block is a square made up of four right-angle triangles, each occupying a quarter of the square. There are several popular QST variations, such as Hourglass block which uses two identical HSTs to create two identical hourglass shapes (used in Starbound Quilt, page 92). This quilt uses the split quarter-square triangle, which is made of one HST and two right-angle triangles. This method produces 2 different blocks that are mirror images of one another. For a refresher on sewing HSTS, see Stepping Stones Quilt (page 34).

MATERIALS

Yardages are based on 42″-wide fabric.

Fabric A: 2 yards

Accent Fabric Group B: ⅝ yard each of 6 colors

Accent Fabric Group C: ⅝ yard each of 6 colors

Binding: ⅝ yard

Backing: 4⅝ yards

Batting: 82″ × 82″

Fabric

For this quilt, I used Riley Blake Confetti Cotton in Purple, Pink Dogwood, Amethyst, Songbird, Sunshine, Cinnamon, Frosting, Super Pink, Periwinkle, Timberline, Canary, Beehive, and Cloud.

Finished Project: 74˝ × 74˝
Skill Level: Beginner
Skill Builder: Sewing Quarter-Square Triangles

CUTTING

Fabric A (Cloud)

Cut 4 strips 6½˝ × WOF, subcut into:

- **A1:** 24 squares 6½˝ × 6½˝

Cut 16 strips 2½˝ × WOF, sew together and subcut into:

- **A2:** 7 strips 2½˝ × 70½˝
- **A3:** 2 strips 2½˝ × 74½˝

Accent Fabric Group B

From each of 6 Accent Group B Fabrics:

Cut 1 strips 6½˝ × WOF, subcut into:

- **B1:** 4 squares 6½˝ × 6½˝

Cut 2 strips 5½˝ × WOF, subcut into:

- **B2:** 14 squares 5½˝ × 5½˝

Accent Fabric Group C

From each of 6 Accent Group C Fabrics:

Cut 2 strips 6¼˝ × WOF, subcut into:

- **C1:** 7 squares 6¼˝ × 6¼˝

Binding

Cut 8 strips 2¼˝ × WOF.

FABRIC

A

Colorway	Accent Group B	Accent Group C
1		
2		
3		
4		
5		
6		

CONSTRUCTION

Seam allowances are ¼˝ unless otherwise noted.

Quarter-Square Triangle Units

Decide which color from Accent Group B to pair with a color from Accent Group C. Set aside the fabric for Accent Group C.

1. Draw a diagonal line on the wrong side of all A1 squares. Place an A1 square on top of a B1 square RST. Sew a ¼˝ seam on both sides from the drawn line. Cut on the line. ***fig. A***

2. Press the seam toward the accent fabric. Do not trim. Call this A1B1 HST Unit. ***fig. B***

3. Repeat Steps 1–2 with all of A1 squares and B1 squares. You should have a total of 48 A1B1 HST Units, 8 units in each of the 6 colorways. We will use only 7 A1B1 HST Units from each colorway, so save the extras for future projects. ***fig. C***

A

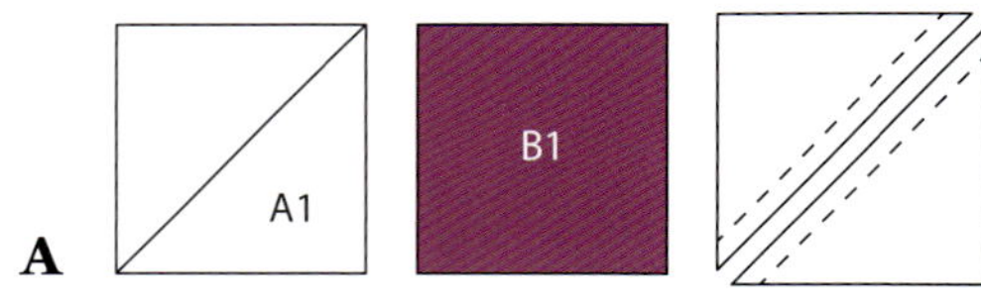

B

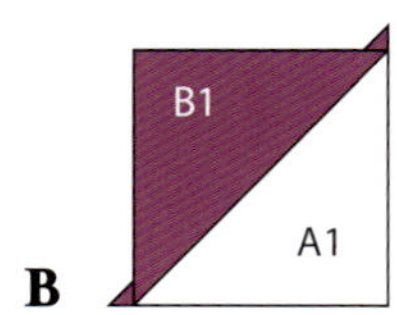

C

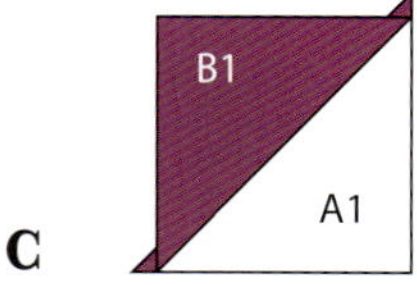

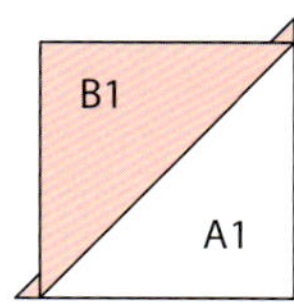

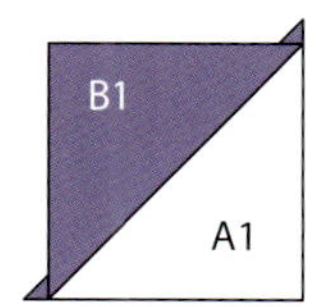

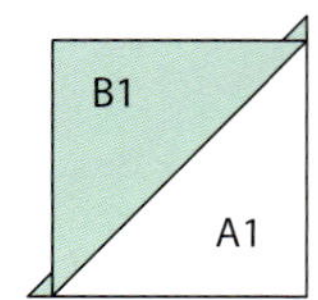

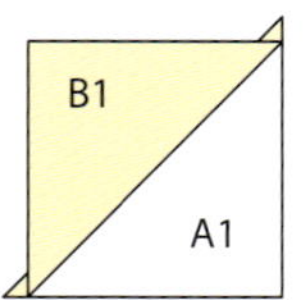

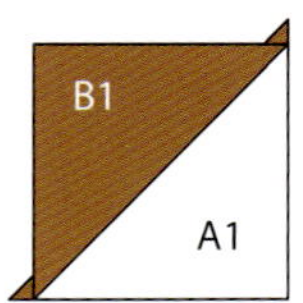

A1B1 HST Units

4. Draw a diagonal line on the wrong side of a set C1 squares. Center a C1 square on top of a coordinating A1B1 HST Unit. Note that the C1 square may not align perfectly with the A1B1 HST, but there will be plenty of wiggle room for trimming. Placement matters, so ensure each unit is positioned as shown. ***fig. D***

5. Sew a ¼˝ seam on both sides of the drawn line. Cut on the line. ***fig. E***

6. Press the seams open, and trim to 5½˝ × 5½˝. Note that this yields 2 different Quarter-Square Triangles (QST). Call these QST-A units and QST-B units. ***fig. F***

7. Repeat Steps 4–6 with all C1 squares and coordinating A1B1 HST Units. You should have a total of 42 QST-A Units and 42 QST-B Units. ***fig. G***

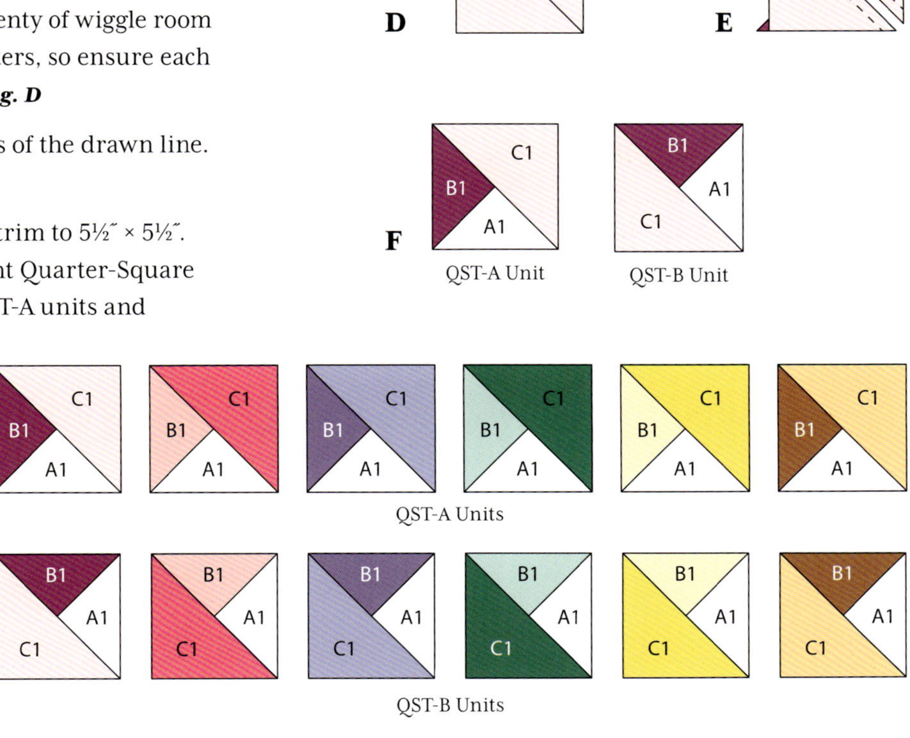

Make Unit A and Unit B

1. Sew a Unit QST-A Unit to the left side of a coordinating B2 square as shown. Press the seam toward the B2 square. Call this Unit A. Repeat to make a total of 7 Units A from Colorway 1. ***fig. H***

2. Repeat Step 1 with all of QST-A Units and coordinating B2 squares. You should have 42 Unit A, 7 units from each colorway. ***fig. I***

H

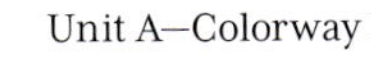

Unit A—Colorway 1

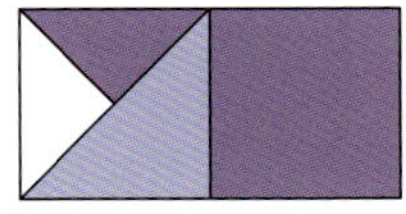

Unit A—Colorway 2

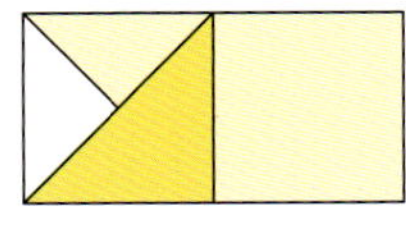

Unit A—Colorway 3

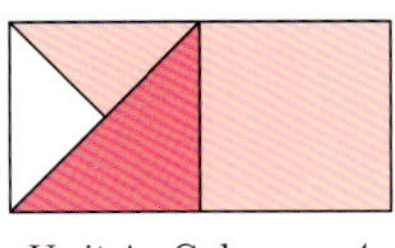

Unit A—Colorway 4

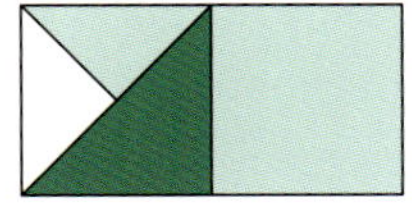

Unit A—Colorway 5

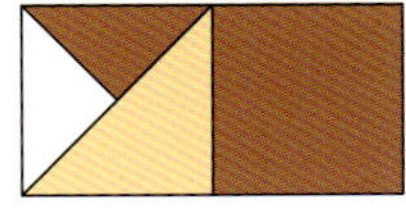

Unit A—Colorway 6

I

3. Sew a Unit QST-B Unit to the right side of a coordinating B2 square. Press the seam toward the B2 square. Call this Unit B. Repeat to make a total of 7 Unit B from Colorway 1. ***fig. J***

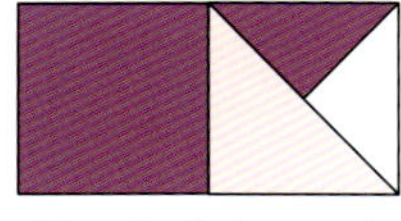

J

Unit B—Colorway 1

4. Repeat Step 3 with all of QST-B Units and coordinating B2 squares. You should have 42 Unit B, 7 units from each colorway. ***fig. K***

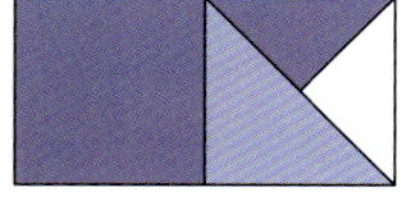

Unit B—Colorway 2

Unit B—Colorway 3

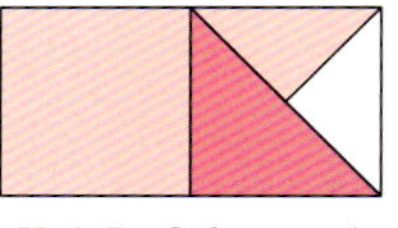

Unit B—Colorway 4

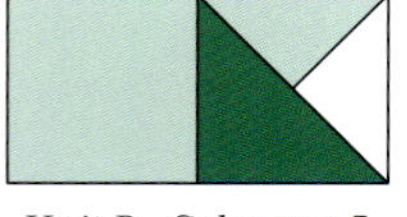

Unit B—Colorway 5

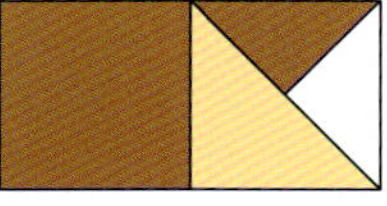

Unit B—Colorway 6

K

Make Column A and Column B

1. Arrange 7 Unit A—Colorway 1 and 7 Unit B—Colorway 1 into a vertical column. Nest the seams as you sew each unit together. Press the seams open or in the same direction. Call this Unit A1. ***fig. L***

2. Repeat Step 1 with Colorway 2 and Colorway 3 to make Unit A2 and Unit A3. Each unit measures 10½″ × 70½″. ***fig. M***

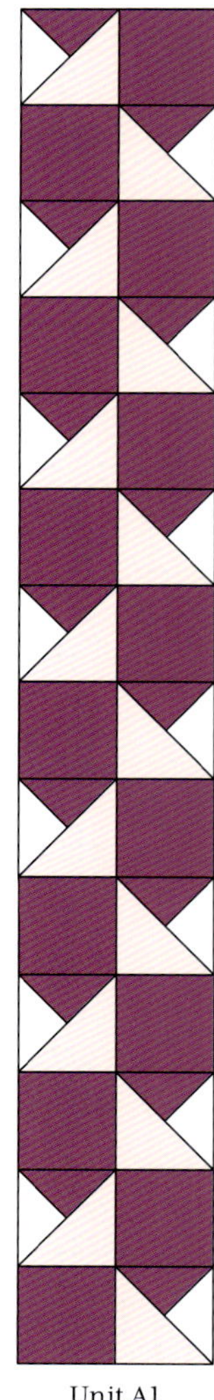

L

Unit A1

M

Unit A2

Unit A3

3. Arrange 7 Unit B—Colorway 4 and 7 Unit A—Colorway 4 into a vertical column. Nest the seams as you sew each unit together. Press the seams open or in the same direction. Call this Unit B1. ***fig. N***

4. Repeat Step 3 with Colorway 5 and Colorway 6 to make Unit B2 and Unit B3. ***fig. O***

Assemble the Quilt

1. Arrange the following units into 13 columns ***(fig. P)***:

   A2 strip, Unit A1, A2 strip, Unit B1, A2 strip, Unit A2, A2 strip, Unit B2, A2 strip, Unit A3, A2 strip, Unit B3

Q

R

2. Sew the columns together. Press the seams toward the A2 strips.

3. Sew 2 A3 strips to the top and bottom of the quilt. ***fig. Q***

4. Press the seams toward A3 strips. The quilt top measures 74½″ × 74½″. ***fig. R***

Finish the Quilt

Layer, quilt, and bind the project as desired. See Quilt Assembly (page 24).

Starbound Quilt

Starbound is constructed by setting the blocks on point, which means rotating them 45 degrees rather than following a traditional grid layout. To make this work, you'll add triangles to the sides of each row to fill in the gaps created by the rotated blocks. This design also uses quarter-square triangles, which are a great progression of HSTs.

Sewing On-Point Blocks

If you're new to working with an on-point quilt, starting with the larger blocks in this project will give you more room for error and make the process a bit easier. Pressing and using starch can also be helpful, especially when working with the bias edges of the triangles. Starching the fabric before cutting and pressing helps stabilize those edges, making it easier to sew them to the rows without stretching the fabric.

MATERIALS

Yardages are based on 42″-wide fabric.

Fabric A: 2 yards

Fabric B: 1 yard

Fabric C: 1 yard

Fabric D: 1⅜ yards

Binding: ½ yard

Backing: 4¼ yards

Batting: 76″ × 76″

Fabric

In this quilt, I used Riley Blake Confetti Cotton in Bear Lake, Bleached Denim, Cloud, and Dainty Daisy in Navy.

Finished Project: 68˝ × 68˝
Skill Level: Intermediate
Skill Builder: Sewing On Point

CUTTING

FABRIC	
A	B
C	D

Fabric A (Cloud)

Cut 3 strips 12½″ × WOF, subcut into:

- **A1:** 36 strips 3½″ × 12½″

Cut 2 strips 5½″ × WOF, subcut into:

- **A2:** 9 squares 5½″ × 5½″

Cut 4 strips 4½″ × WOF, subcut into:

- **A3:** 36 squares 4½″ × 4½″

Fabric B (Bear Lake)

Cut 3 strips 5½″ × WOF, subcut into:

- **B1:** 18 squares 5½″ × 5½″

Cut 3 strips 4½″ × WOF, subcut into:

- **B2:** 25 squares 4½″ × 4½″

Fabric C (Navy)

Cut 2 strips 5½″ × WOF, subcut into:

- **C1:** 9 squares 5½″ × 5½″
- **C2:** 2 squares 4½″ × 4½″

Cut 2 strips 4½″ × WOF, subcut into:

- **C2:** 18 squares 4½″ × 4½″ (total of 20)

Cut 2 strips 3½″ × WOF, subcut into:

- **C3:** 24 squares 3½″ × 3½″

Fabric D (Bleached Denim)

Cut 2 strips 22½″ × WOF; from each strip, subcut:

- **D2:** 1 square 22½″ × 22½″
- **D1:** 1 square 13⅝″ × 13⅝″

Binding

Cut 7 strips 2¼″ × width of fabric (WOF).

CONSTRUCTION

Seam allowances are ¼″ unless otherwise noted.

Ohio Star Blocks

1. Draw a diagonal line on the wrong side of all B1 squares. Place a B1 square on top of an A2 square RST. Sew a ¼″ seam on both sides of the drawn line. Cut on the line. ***fig. A***

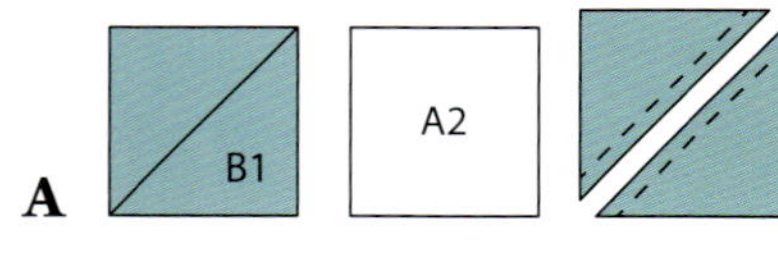

2. Press the seam toward the B1 square. Do not trim. Call this B1A2 HST Unit. Repeat with the 8 remaining A2 squares to make a total of 18 B1A2 HST Units. ***fig. B***

3. Repeat Steps 1–2 to make a total of 18 B1C1 HST units by pairing 9 B1 squares with 9 C1 squares. ***fig. C***

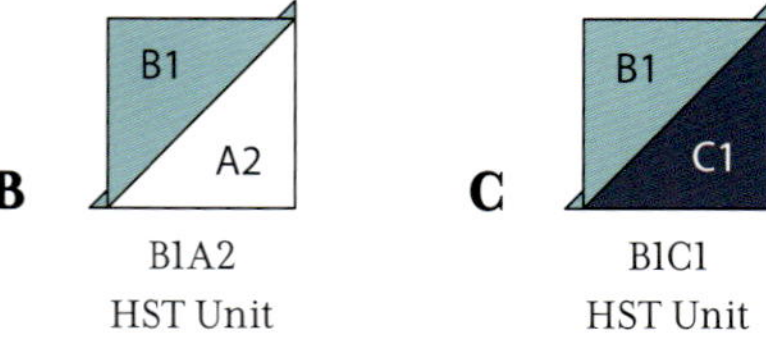

B1A2 HST Unit

B1C1 HST Unit

4. Draw a diagonal line on the wrong side of all of B1A2 HST Units, opposite the seam. Center a B1A2 HST Unit on top of a B1C1 HST Unit, RST. Note that they may not align perfectly, but there will be plenty of wiggle room for trimming. Placement matters, so ensure each unit is positioned as shown. ***fig. D***

5. Sew a ¼″ seam on both sides of the drawn line. Cut on the line. ***fig. E***

6. Press the seam open and trim to 4½″ × 4½″. Call this QST Unit. Repeat to make a total of 36 QST Units. ***fig. F***

7. Arrange the following units into 3 rows:

Row 1: A3 square, QST Unit, A3 square

Row 2: QST Unit, B2 square, QST Unit

Row 3: A3 square, QST Unit, A3 square

9. Sew the units into rows, and press the seams away from QST Units. Sew the rows together, and press the seams open. The Ohio Star Block measures 12½″ × 12½″. Repeat to make a total of 9 Ohio Star Blocks. ***fig. H***

F

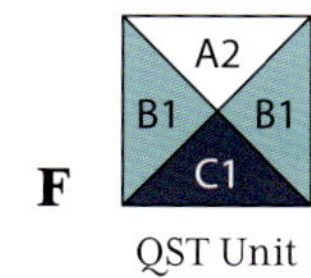

QST Unit

G

H

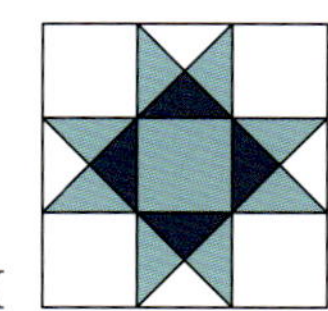

I

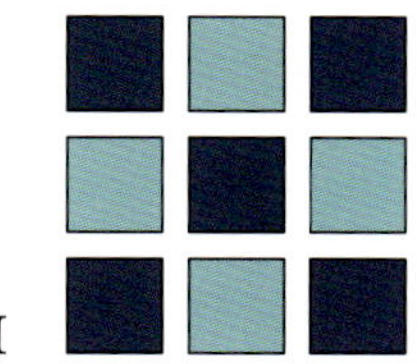

J

Nine Patch Block

Nine Patch Blocks

1. Arrange the following units into 3 rows (***fig. I***):

Row 1: C2 square, B2 square, C2 square

Row 2: B2 square, C2 square, B2 square

Row 3: C2 square, B2 square, C2 square

2. Sew the units into rows, and press the seams toward C2 squares. Sew the rows together, and press the seams open. The Nine Patch Block measures 12½″ × 12½″. ***fig. J***

3. Repeat Steps 1 and 2 to make a total of 4 Nine Patch Blocks.

Assemble the Strips

1. Arrange the following units into 2 rows (***fig. K***):

Row 1: C3 square, A1 strip, C3 square

Row 2: A1 strip, Ohio Star Block, A1 strip

2. Sew the units into rows, and press the seams toward A1 strips. Sew the rows together, and press the seam open. Call this Strip 1. Repeat Steps 1 and 2 to make a second unit. ***fig. L***

K

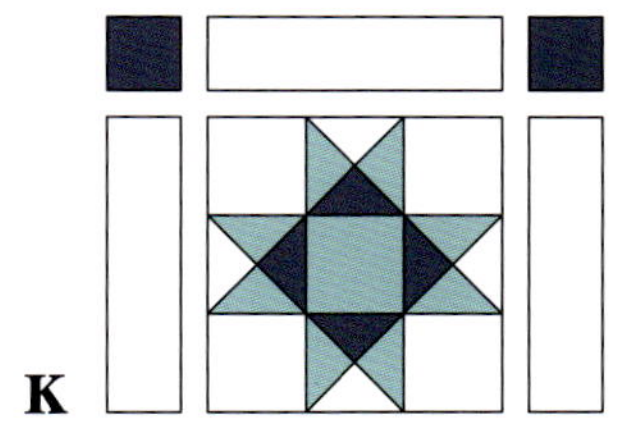

L

Strip 1

3. Arrange the following units into 2 rows (***fig. M***):

Row 1: C3 square, A1 strip, C3 square, A1 strip, C3 square, A1 strip, C3 square

Row 2: A1 strip, Ohio Star Block, A1 strip, Nine Patch Block, A1 strip, Ohio Star Block, A1 strip

M

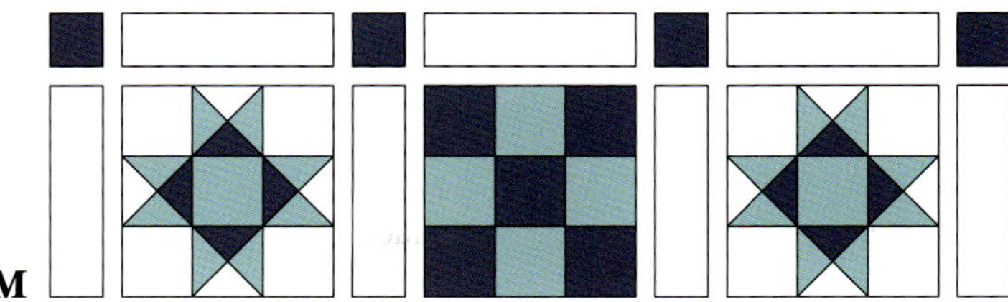

4. Sew the units into rows, and press the seams toward the A1 strips. Sew the rows together, and press the seam open. Call this Strip 2. Repeat Steps 3 and 4 to make a second unit. ***fig. N***

5. Arrange the following units into 3 rows ***(fig. O)***:

Row 1: C3 square, A1 strip, C3 square, A1 strip, C3 square, A1 strip, C3 square, A1 strip, C3 square, A1 strip, C3 square

Row 2: A1 strip, Ohio Star Block, A1 strip, Nine Patch Block, A1 strip, Ohio Star Block, A1 strip, Nine Patch Block, A1 strip, Ohio Star Block, A1 strip

Row 3: C3 square, A1 strip, C3 square, A1 strip, C3 square, A1 strip, C3 square, A1 strip, C3 square, A1 strip, C3 square

6. Sew the units into rows, and press the seams toward A1 strips. Sew the rows together, and press the seams open. Call this Strip 3. ***fig. P***

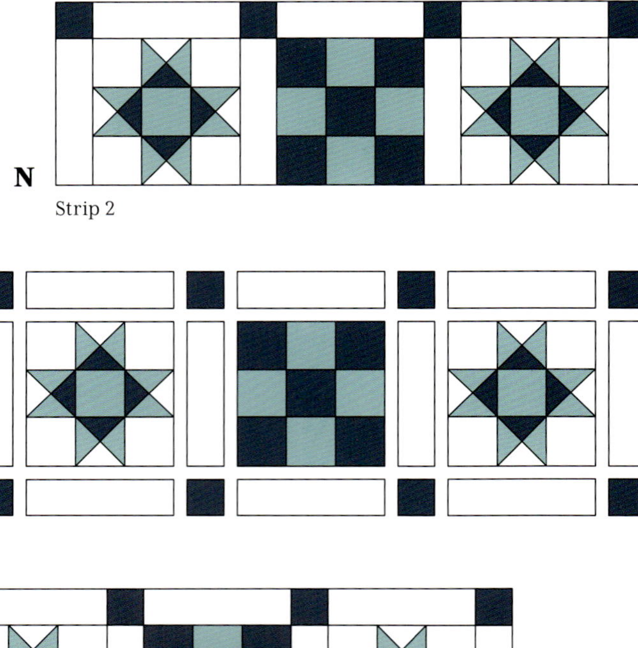

N

Strip 2

O

P

Strip 3

Assemble the Quilt

1. Cut each D1 square from corner to corner diagonally. Cut each D2 square twice diagonally. ***fig. Q***

Q

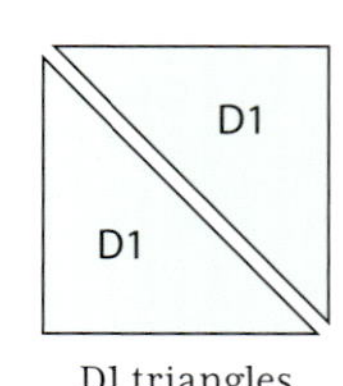

D1 triangles

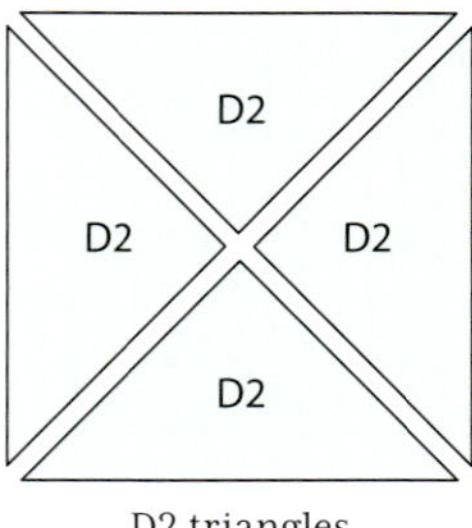

D2 triangles

2. Arrange the units into 7 diagonal rows. ***fig. R***

3. Align the straight edges as you sew the units into rows. Note that the triangle pieces should overlap the C3 square by ¼˝. Press the seams away from the triangles.

4. Sew the rows together. Press the seams open. The quilt top measures 68˝ × 68˝. ***fig. S***

Finish the Quilt

Layer, quilt, and bind the project as desired. See Quilt Assembly (page 24).

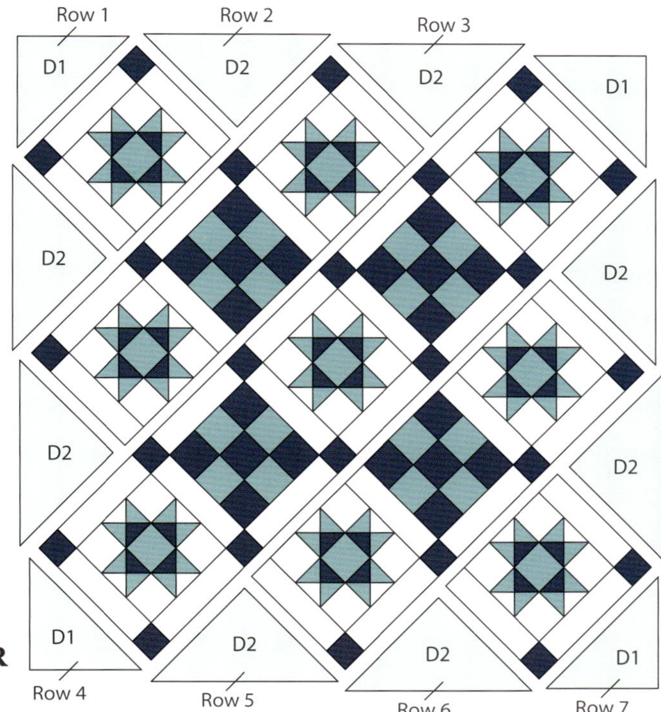

R

S

Butterfly Blossoms Quilt

There's something so satisfying about sewing an Orange Peel block. Its gentle curves and timeless simplicity make it one of those designs that never goes out of style. As I worked on this Butterfly Blossom Quilt, I couldn't help but notice how the curves came together like delicate petals or butterfly wings, soft and full of movement. That's where the name came from. This quilt feels like a garden in full bloom, with butterflies gently fluttering through it.

Sewing Orange Peel Blocks

Once you've conquered the quarter-circle blocks in the Bloomer Quilt (page 48), sewing Orange Peel blocks will feel very familiar. The trick is all in finding the center of your pieces and pinning the 3 key spots: center and both ends. Once you have that down, it's all about easing the curves together. I've designed the templates with just enough wiggle room to make trimming easy and stress-free.

MATERIALS

Yardages are based on 42″-wide fabric.

Fabric A: 4⅝ yards

Accent B–F: 1 yard each of 5 colors

Binding: ⅝ yard

Backing: 4½ yards

Batting: 78″ × 78″

Fabric

For this quilt, I used Riley Blake Blossom in Aqua, Baby Pink, Honey, Silver, Blossom On White Spring, and Dapple Dot in Marmalade.

Finished Project: 70˝ × 70˝
Skill Level: Intermediate
Skill Builder: Sewing Orange Peel Blocks

CUTTING

To access the templates, go to Templates (page 124). For this project, you need Template C and Template E. Refer to the cutting diagrams to most efficiently cut the templates from the fabric.

Fabric A (Blossom On White Spring)

Cut 11 strips 8¾″ × WOF, subcut into:

- **A1:** 104 Template E

Cut 8 strips 7½″ × WOF, subcut into:

- **A2:** 48 Template C

Fabric B (Aqua)

Cut 2 strips 8¾″ × WOF, subcut into:

- **B1:** 16 Template E

Cut 2 strips 7½″ × WOF, subcut into:

- **B2:** 12 Template C

Fabric C (Baby Pink)

Cut 3 strips 8¾″ × WOF, subcut into:

- **C1:** 24 Template E
- **C2:** 2 Template C

Cut 1 strip 7½″ × WOF, subcut into:

- **C2:** 6 Template C (total of 8)

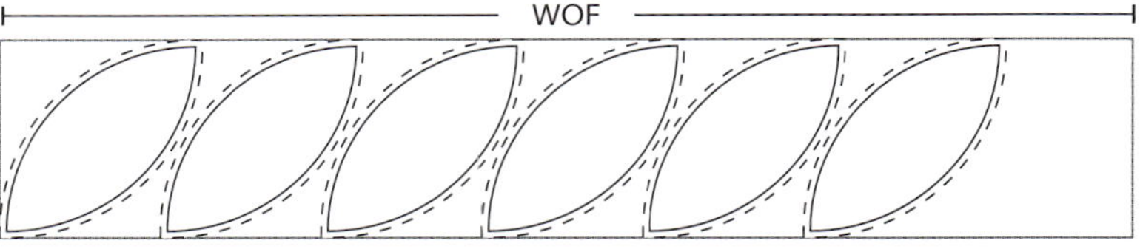

Cutting template C

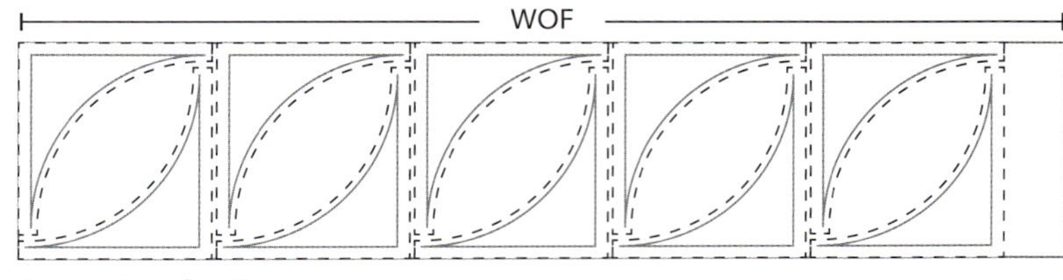

Cutting template E

Fabric D (Honey)

Cut 2 strips 8¾″ × WOF, subcut into:

- **D1:** 16 Template E

Cut 2 strips 7½″ × WOF, subcut into:

- **D2:** 12 Template C

Fabric E (Marmalade)

Cut 3 strips 8¾″ × WOF, subcut into:

- **E1:** 24 Template E
- **E2:** 2 Template C

Cut 1 strip 7½″ × WOF, subcut into:

- **E2:** 6 Template C (total of 8)

Fabric F (Silver)

Cut 2 strips 8¾″ × WOF, subcut into:

- **F1:** 16 Template E

Cut 2 strips 7½″ × WOF, subcut into

- **F2:** 12 Template C

Binding

Cut into 8 strips 2¼″ × width of fabric (WOF).

CONSTRUCTION

Seam allowances are ¼˝ unless otherwise noted.

Orange Peel Blocks

1. Pair an A1 with a B2. Fold each piece in half to create a crease. ***fig. A***

2. Place the A1 on the B2 RST, lining up the creases. ***fig. B***

3. Pin at the center point, then the edges. Pin as often as desired, using more pins if you are new to sewing curves. Sew with a ¼˝ seam along the curve, carefully adjust the fabric as needed. Press the seam toward A1. ***fig. C***

4. Fold an A1 in half to create a crease. Place on top of the other edge of B2, RST. ***fig. D***

5. Pin the pieces together, ensuring that the A1 piece overlaps the B2 piece by ¼˝ at both ends. Note that the edges will not align perfectly, but you'll have wiggle room for trimming later. ***fig. E***

6. Press the seam toward A1, and trim to 7½˝ × 7½˝. Make sure that you have a ¼˝ seam allowance on each side of the curve. Call this A1B2 Block. ***fig. F***

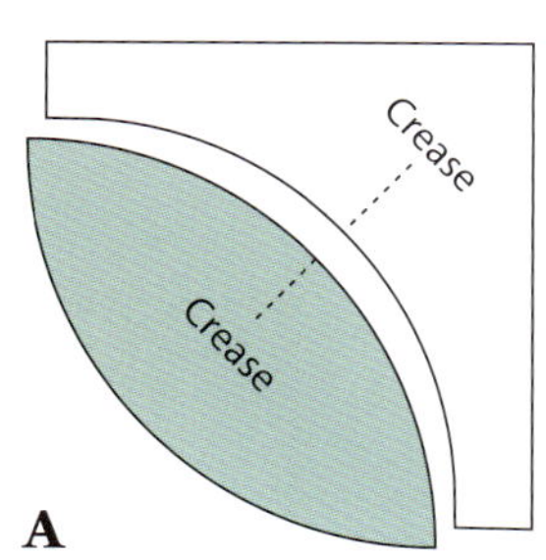

A

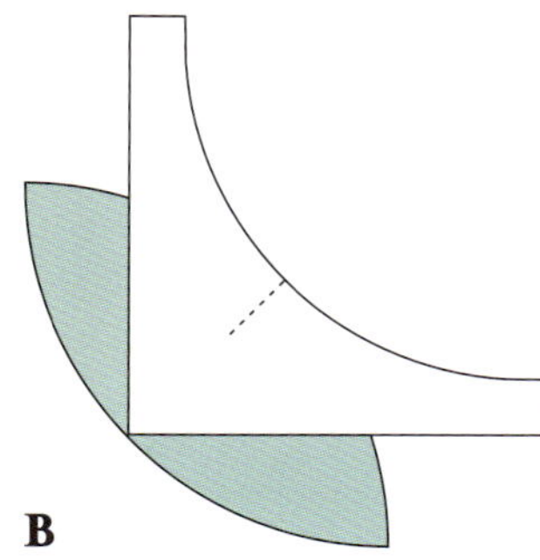

B

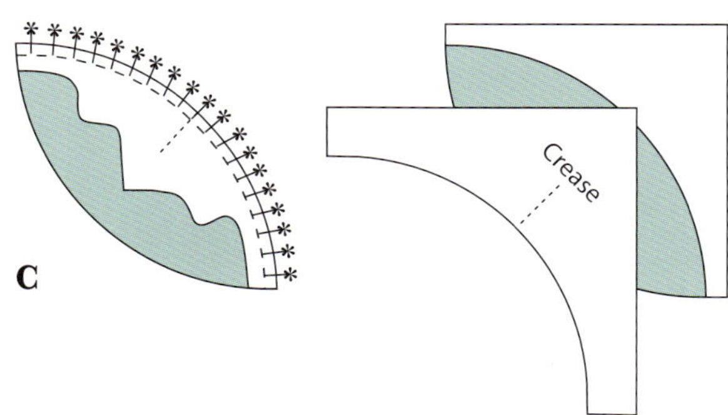

C

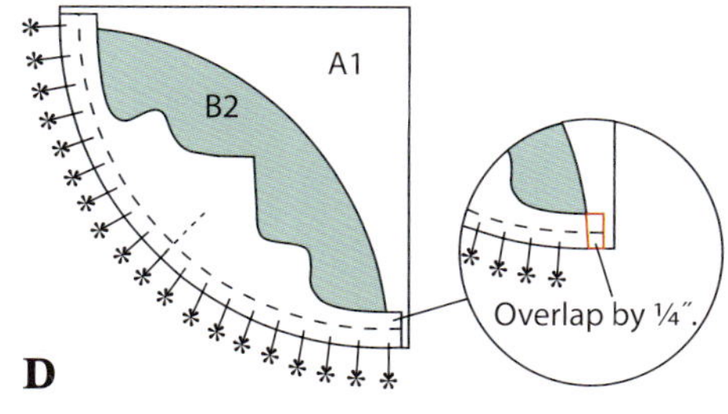

D

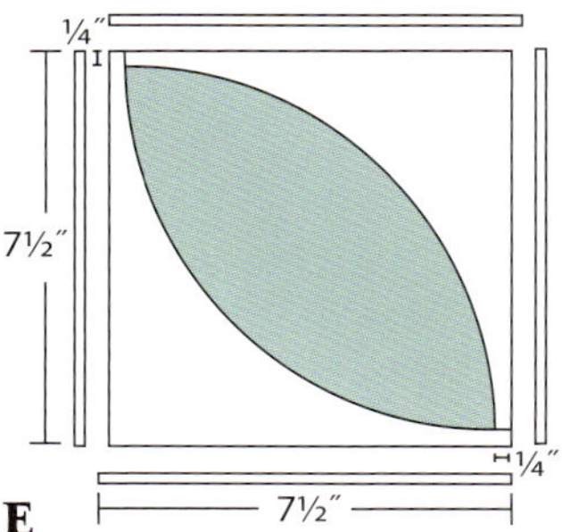

E

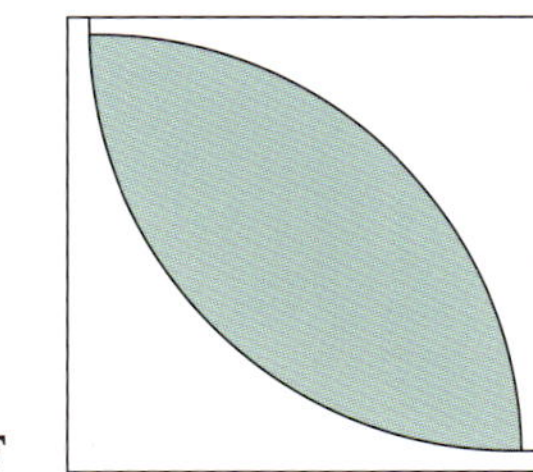

F

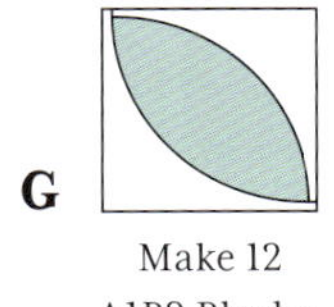

G

Make 12
A1B2 Blocks.

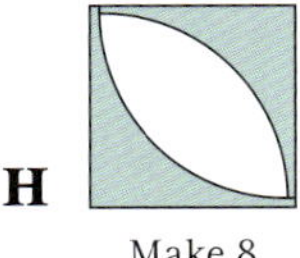

H

Make 8
A2B1 Blocks.

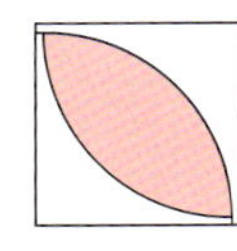

I

Make 8
A1C2 Blocks.

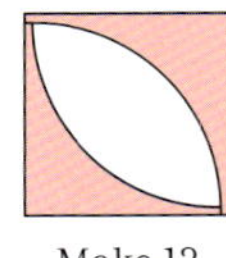

J

Make 12
A2C1 Blocks.

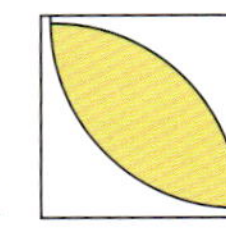

K

Make 12
A1D2 Blocks.

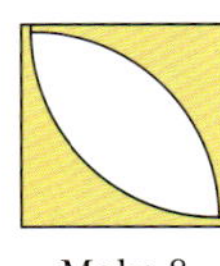

L

Make 8
A2D1 Blocks.

M

Make 8
A1E2 Blocks.

N

Make 12
A2E1 Blocks.

O

Make 12
A1F2 Blocks.

P

Make 8
A2F1 Blocks.

7. Repeat Steps 1–6 to make a total of 12 A1B2 Blocks. For half of the blocks, press the seams toward A1. For the remaining half, press the seams toward B2. This will ensure that the seams nest properly when assembling the Butterfly Blocks. ***fig. G***

8. Use the same method in Steps 1–6 to make the following units:

Pair 8 A2 with 16 B1 to make 8 A2B1 Blocks. ***fig. H***

Pair 16 A1 with 8 C2 to make 8 A1C2 Blocks. ***fig. I***

Pair 12 A2 with 24 C1 to make 12 A2C1 Blocks. ***fig. J***

Pair 24 A1 with 12 D2 to make 12 A1D2 Blocks. ***fig. K***

Pair 8 A2 with 16 D1 to make 8 A2D1 Blocks. ***fig. L***

Pair 16 A1 with 8 E2 to make 8 Unit A1E2. ***fig. M***

Pair 12 A2 with 24 E1 to make 12 A2E1 Blocks. ***fig. N***

Pair 24 A1 with 12 F2 to make 12 A1F2 Blocks. ***fig. O***

Pair 8 A2 with 16 F1 to make 8 A2F1 Blocks. ***fig. P***

Butterfly Blocks

1. Arrange 4 A1B2 Blocks into 2 rows. ***fig. Q***

2. Nest the seams as you sew the rows together. Pay close attention to the orientation of each unit. Press the seams open.

3. Sew the rows together. Press the seams open. Call this A1B2 Butterfly Block. Repeat to make a total of 3 blocks. ***fig. R***

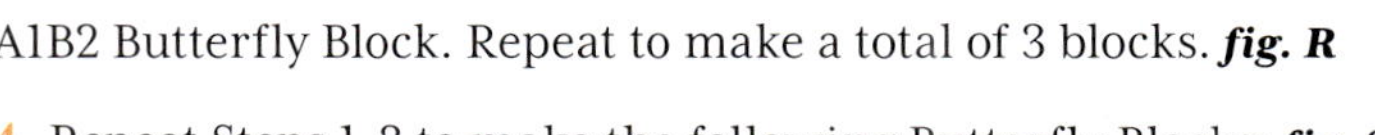

Q

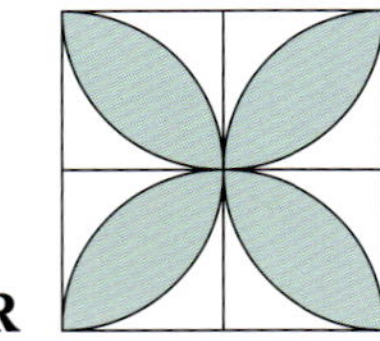

R

4. Repeat Steps 1–3 to make the following Butterfly Blocks: ***fig. S***

Make 2
A2B1 Butterfly Blocks.

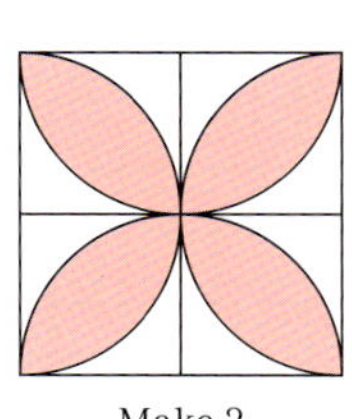

Make 2
A1C2 Butterfly Blocks.

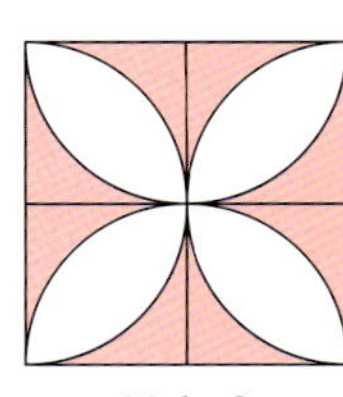

Make 3
A2C1 Butterfly Blocks.

Make 3
A1D2 Butterfly Blocks.

Make 2
A2D1 Butterfly Blocks.

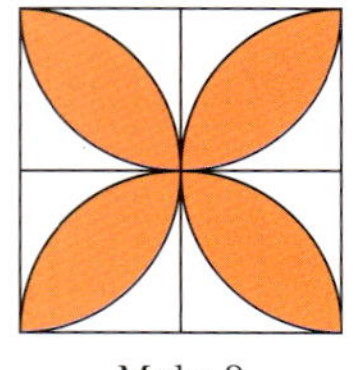

Make 2
A1E2 Butterfly Blocks.

Make 3
A2E1 Butterfly Blocks.

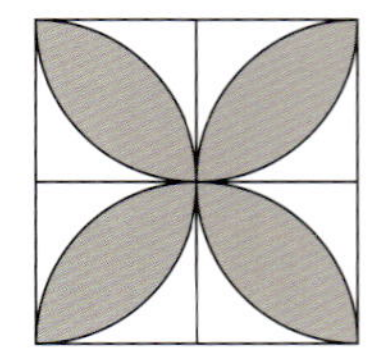

Make 3
A1F2 Butterfly Blocks.

Make 2
A2F1 Butterfly Blocks.

S

Assemble the Quilt

1. Arrange the Butterfly Blocks into 5 vertical columns ***(fig. T)***:

Column 1: A1B2, A2B1, A1B2, A2B1, A1B2

Column 2: A2C1, A1C2, A2C1, A1C2, A2C1

Column 3: A1D2, A2D1, A1D2, A2D1, A1D2

Column 4: A2E1, A1E2, A2E1, A1E2, A2E1

Column 5: A1F2, A2F1, A1F2, A2F1, A1F2

2. Sew the units into columns. Press the seams open. ***fig. U***

3. Sew the columns together. Press the seams open. The quilt top measures 70½″ × 70½″. ***fig. V***

Finish the Quilt

Layer, quilt, and bind the project as desired. See Quilt Assembly (page 24).

T

U

V

Cozy Cabin Quilt

Have you ever worked on a quilt that surprised you at every turn? That's exactly how I felt while designing this pattern. A traditional log cabin block is a reminder of why we fell in love with quilting in the first place. A Log Cabin is like a blank canvas: it can be soft and subtle, bold and modern, or cozy and traditional. The Cozy Cabin Quilt is an ideal pattern for beginners thanks to its straightforward construction. And, if you're looking to make a dent in your fabric stash, this quilt is the perfect way to use up all those scraps.

Sewing Log Cabin Blocks

The Log Cabin quilt block is a classic quilt block that begins with a square, symbolizing the heart or hearth of a cabin. The square is surrounded by "logs" which are the strips of fabric added to the starting square in a clockwise or counterclockwise spiral around the center.

Here are some helpful tips for making a Log Cabin Quilt Block:

- Precision cutting is the key to avoiding wonky blocks.
- Pressing seams as you go (with an iron or seam roller) will keep the block nice and crisp.
- Try chain piecing to save time when making multiple blocks.
- A ¼″ seam allowance is crucial to ensure that your blocks fit together perfectly.

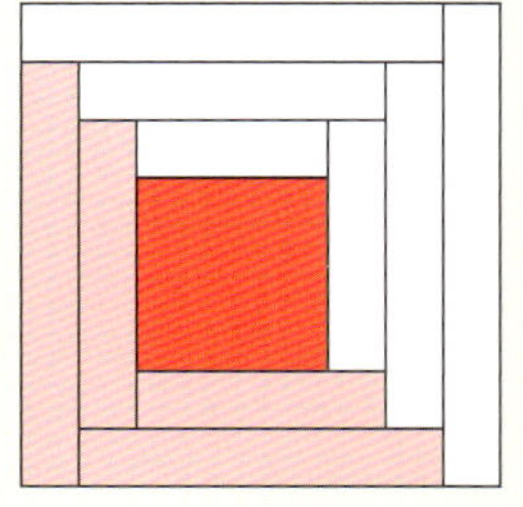

Log Cabin Block

MATERIALS

Yardages are based on 42″-wide fabric. Fat Quarter (FQ) measures 18″ × 21″.

Fabric A: 3⅛ yards

Accent Fabric Group B: 1 FQ each of 4 colors

Accent Fabric Group C: ⅝ yard each of 4 colors

Binding: ⅝ yard

Backing: 4⅝ yards

Batting: 83″ × 83″

Fabric

For this quilt, I used Riley Blake Dapple Dot in Asparagus, Autumn, Aqua, Frosting, Marmalade, Dapple Dot on White Rainbow, Bee Cross Stitch in Riley Teal, Cayenne, and Leaf.

Finished Project: 75˝ × 75˝
Skill Level: Advanced Beginner
Skill Builder: Sewing Log Cabin Blocks

CUTTING

Fabric A (Dapple Dot on White Rainbow)

Cut 53 strips 2″ × WOF, subcut into:

- **A1:** 36 strips 2″ × 13″
- **A2:** 36 strips 2″ × 11½″
- **A3:** 36 strips 2″ × 10″
- **A4:** 36 strips 2″ × 8½″
- **A5:** 36 strips 2″ × 7″
- **A6:** 36 strips 2″ × 5½″

Accent Fabric Group B

From each of 4 fabrics:

Cut 9 strips 2″ × WOF, subcut into:

- **B1:** 9 squares 5½″ × 5½″

FABRIC		
	A	
Colorway	Accent Group B	Accent Group C
1		
2		
3		
4		

Accent Fabric Group C

From each of 4 fabrics, cut:

- **C1:** 9 strips 2″ × 11½″
- **C2:** 9 strips 2″ × 10″
- **C3:** 9 strips 2″ × 8½″
- **C4:** 9 strips 2″ × 7″

Binding

Cut 8 strips 2¼″ × width of fabric (WOF).

CONSTRUCTION

Log Cabin Blocks

1. Arrange the following units around a B1 square as shown. ***fig. A***

2. Sew the units to the starting square. The numbers indicate the order in which to add the strips. Press the seams away from the starting square. The finished unit (Unit 1) measures 13″ × 13″. ***fig. B***

3. Repeat Steps 1–2 to make a total of 9 Unit 1s. ***fig. C***

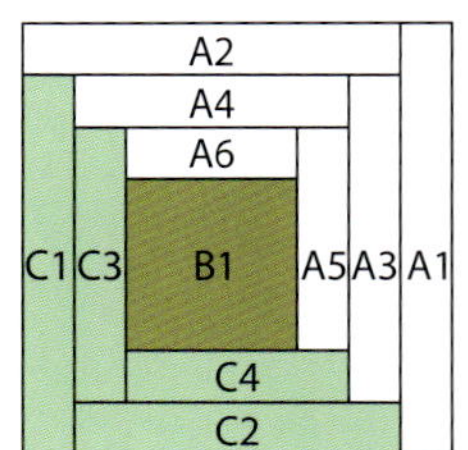

A

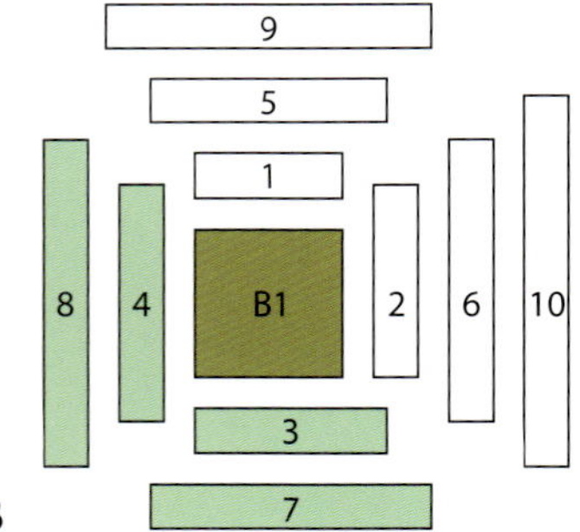

B

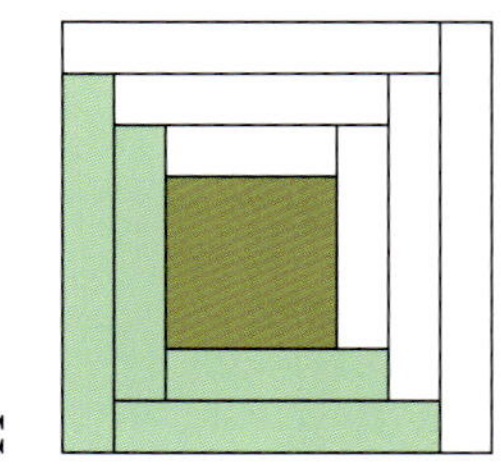
C

4. Repeat Steps 1–2 to make a total of 9 units from each colorway: ***fig. D***

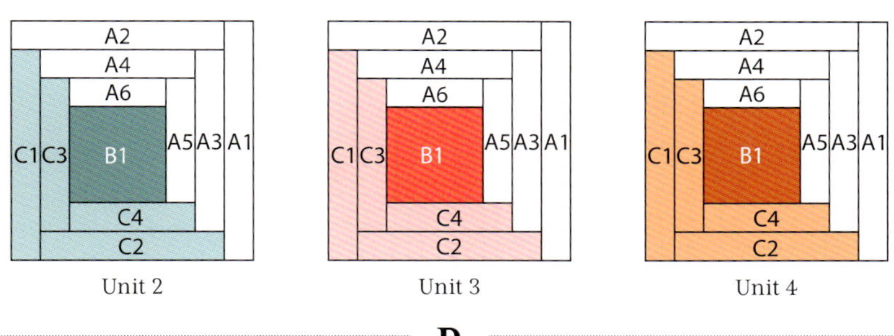

Unit 2 Unit 3 Unit 4

D

Assemble the Quilt

1. Arrange the units into 6 rows, paying close attention to the orientation of each unit ***(fig. E)***:

Row 1: Unit 1, Unit 3, Unit 2, Unit 4, Unit 1, Unit 3

Row 2: Unit 4, Unit 2, Unit 3, Unit 1, Unit 4, Unit 2

Row 3: Unit 2, Unit 4, Unit 1, Unit 3, Unit 2, Unit 4

Row 4: Unit 3, Unit 1, Unit 4, Unit 2, Unit 3, Unit 1

Row 5: Unit 1, Unit 3, Unit 2, Unit 4, Unit 1, Unit 3

Row 6: Unit 4, Unit 2, Unit 3, Unit 1, Unit 4, Unit 2

2. Sew the units into rows. Press the seams of Row 1, Row 3, and Row 5 to the right. Press the seams of Row 2, Row 4 and Row 6 to the left.

3. Sew the rows together, nesting the seams. Press the seams open. The quilt top measures 75½″ × 75½″. ***fig. F***

E

F

Alternate Layout Options

These alternate layouts use the same colors and number of blocks as the cover quilt! This is a great pattern for varying the layout, because the real magic happens when you make a quilt your own. Take your time, trust your instincts, and have fun with it.

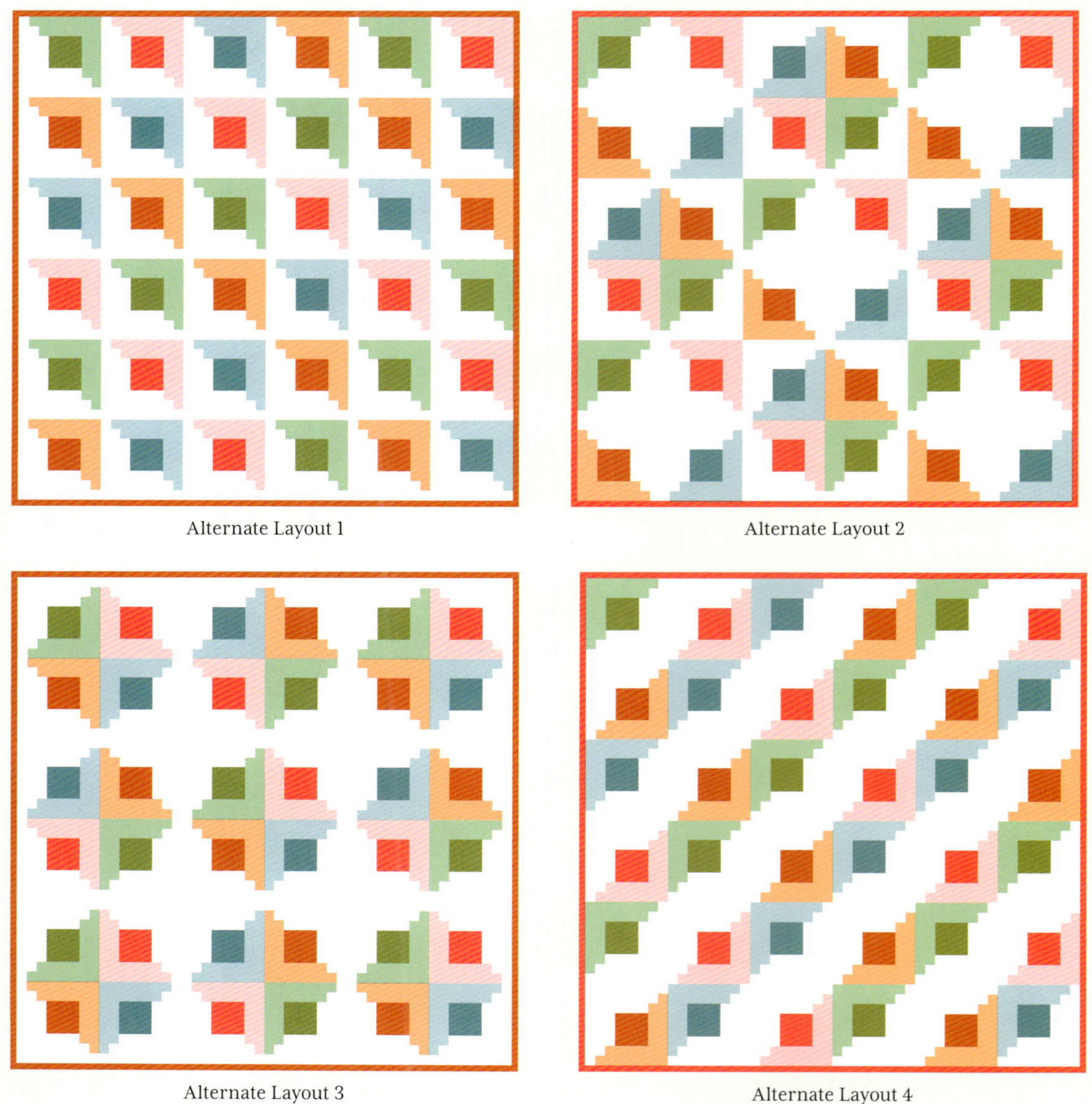

Alternate Layout 1

Alternate Layout 2

Alternate Layout 3

Alternate Layout 4

Finish the Quilt

Layer, quilt, and bind the project as desired. See Quilt Assembly (page 24).

Urban Cottage Quilt

Making the Urban Cottage Quilt feels like building a home, one layer at a time. Each block adds a new element of warmth and character, slowly coming together to create something both familiar and beautiful. With every strip added, the quilt starts to feel like a cozy, lived-in space.

Sewing Log Cabin Blocks

For more on Log Cabin blocks, see the Cozy Cabin Quilt (page 104). This quilt uses a variation called a Half Log Cabin Block, meaning we will add fabric strips to only half of the starting square instead of going all around like a traditional Log Cabin block.

We will also use another variation called a Courthouse Steps Block. The Courthouse Steps Block begins with a center square, then you add the fabric strips in pairs directly opposite each other to create a layered step effect.

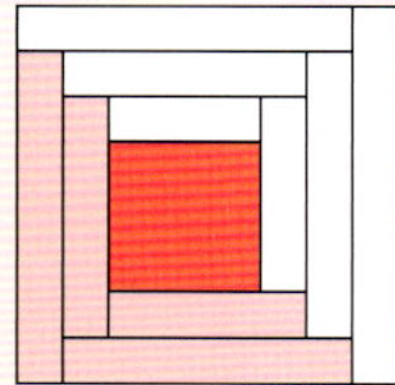

Log Cabin Block

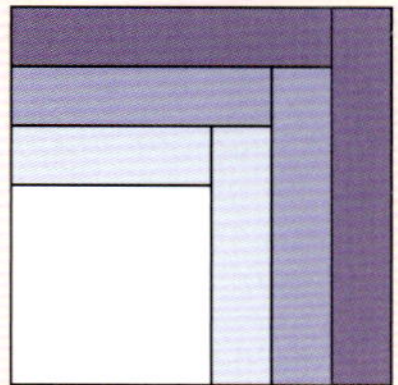

Half Log Cabin Block

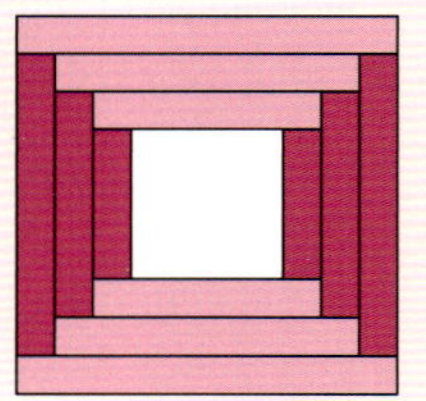

Courthouse Steps Block

Here are some helpful tips for making a Log Cabin Quilt Block:

- Precision cutting is the key to avoiding wonky blocks.
- Pressing seams as you go will keep the block nice and crisp.
- Try chain piecing to save time when making multiple blocks.
- A ¼″ seam allowance is crucial to ensure that your blocks fit together perfectly.

MATERIALS

Yardages are based on 42″-wide fabric. Fat Quarter (FQ) measures 18″ × 21″.

Fabric A: 2⅝ yards

Fabric B: FQ or ¼ yard

Fabric C: ⅜ yard

Fabric D: ½ yard

Fabric E: ⅜ yard

Fabric F: ⅜ yard

Fabric G: ½ yard

Fabric H: ⅜ yard

Fabric J: FQ or ⅜ yard

Fabric K: ½ yard

Binding: ⅝ yard

Backing: 4½ yards

Batting: 80″ × 80″

Fabric (Solids)

For this quilt, I used Riley Blake Dainty Daisy in Mint, Alpine, Jade, Stargazer, Navy, Jazzberry, Waterfall, Dapple Dot in Frosting, Blossom in Peony, and Tone-on-Tone White.

Fabric (Prints)

For this quilt, I used Riley Blake Wanderlust in Main Cream, Main Charcoal, Hawthorn Cream, Hawthorn Curry, Carnation Cream, Carnation Green, Oak Trail Flax, Jasmine Apricot, Sunshine Light Green and Confetti Cotton in Charcoal.

Finished Project: 72˝ × 72˝

Skill Level: Advanced Beginner

Skill Builder: Sewing Half Log Cabin Blocks

CUTTING

FABRIC									
A	B	C	D	E	F	G	H	J	K

Fabric A (Blossom Tone-on-Tone White)

Cut 5 strips 8½″ × WOF, subcut into:

- **A1:** 20 rectangles 8½″ × 4½″
- **A2:** 2 squares 8½″ × 8½″

Sew the leftover fabric strip 8½″ × 16″ together with 2 remaining 8½″ × WOF and subcut into:

- **A3:** 2 strips 8½″ × 48½″

Cut 9 strips 4½″ × WOF, sew 7 together and subcut into:

- **A5:** 2 strips 4½″ × 64½″
- **A6:** 2 strips 4½″ × 72½″

From the remaining 2 strips, subcut:

- **A4:** 4 strips 4½″ × 16½″

Fabric B (Mint)

B1: 8 squares 4½″ × 4½″

B2: 2 rectangles 4½″ × 8½″

Fabric C (Alpine)

Cut 4 strips 2½″ × WOF, subcut into:

- **C1:** 12 rectangles 2½″ × 4½″
- **C2:** 8 rectangles 2½″ × 6½″
- **C3:** 2 rectangles 2½″ × 12½″

Fabric D (Jade)

Cut 5 strips 2½″ × WOF, subcut into:

- **D1:** 12 rectangles 2½″ × 6½″
- **D2:** 8 rectangles 2½″ × 8½″
- **D3:** 2 rectangles 2½″ × 16½″

Fabric E (Aqua)

Cut 2 strips 4½″ × WOF; subcut into:

- **E1:** 12 squares 4½″ × 4½″

Fabric F (Stargazer)

Cut 1 strip 2½″ × WOF, subcut into:

- **F1:** 9 rectangles 2½″ × 4½″

Cut 1 strip 6½″ × WOF, subcut into:

- **F2:** 12 rectangles 6½″ × 2½″
- **F1:** 3 rectangles 2½″ × 4½″ (total of 12)

Fabric G (Navy)

Cut 5 strips 2½″ × WOF, subcut into:

- **G1:** 12 rectangles 2½″ × 6½″
- **G2:** 12 rectangles 2½″ × 8½″

Fabric H (Frosting)

Cut 1 strip 8½″ × WOF, subcut into:

- **H1:** 1 square 8½″ × 8½″
- **H2:** 4 rectangles 8½″ × 4½″

Fabric J (Peony)

Cut 4 strips 2½″ × WOF, subcut into:

- **J1:** 8 rectangles 2½″ × 4½″
- **J2:** 2 rectangles 2½″ × 8½″
- **J3:** 6 rectangles 2½″ × 12½″

Fabric K (Jazzberry)

Cut 5 strips 2½″ × WOF, subcut into:

- **K1:** 8 rectangles 2½″ × 6½″
- **K2:** 2 rectangles 2½″ × 12½″
- **K3:** 6 rectangles 2½″ × 16½″

Binding

Cut 8 strips 2¼″ × width of fabric (WOF).

CONSTRUCTION

Seam allowances are ¼˝ unless otherwise noted.

Half Log Cabin Blocks

1. Sew a C1 rectangle to the top of a B1 square. Press the seam toward the C1 rectangle. Sew a C2 rectangle to the right side of the unit. Press the seam toward the C2 rectangle. ***fig. A***

2. Sew a D1 rectangle to the top of the Step 1 unit. Press the seam toward the D1 rectangle. Sew a D2 rectangle to the right side of the unit. Press the seam toward the D2 rectangle. Call this Unit A1, measuring 8½˝ × 8½˝. ***fig. B***

3. Repeat Steps 1–2 to make a total of 8 Unit A1s.

4. Gather 12 E1 squares, 12 F1, F2, G1 and G2 rectangles. Arrange them as shown and Repeat Steps 1–2 to make a total of 12 Unit B1s. Unit B1 measures 8½˝ × 8½˝. ***fig. C***

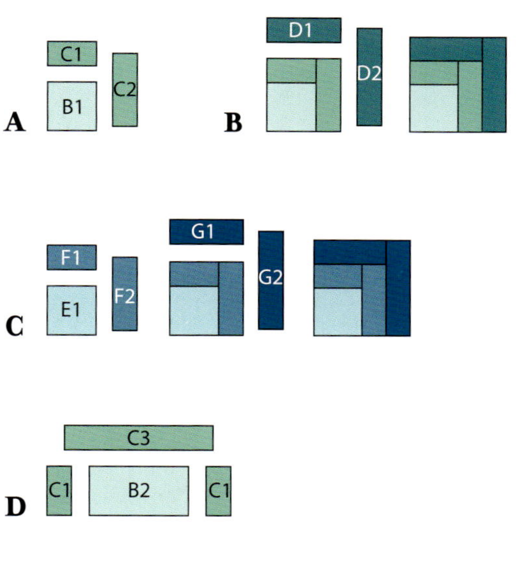

Courthouse Steps Blocks

1. Sew 2 C1 rectangles to 2 sides of a B2 rectangle. Press each seam toward the C1 rectangle. Sew a C3 rectangle to the top side of the unit. Press the seam toward the C3 rectangle. ***fig. D***

2. Sew 2 D1 rectangles to 2 sides of the unit made in Step 1. Press each seam toward the D1 rectangles. Sew a D3 rectangle to the top of the unit. Press the seam toward the D3 rectangle. Call this Unit A2, measuring 8½˝ × 16½˝. Repeat to make the second Unit A2. ***fig. E***

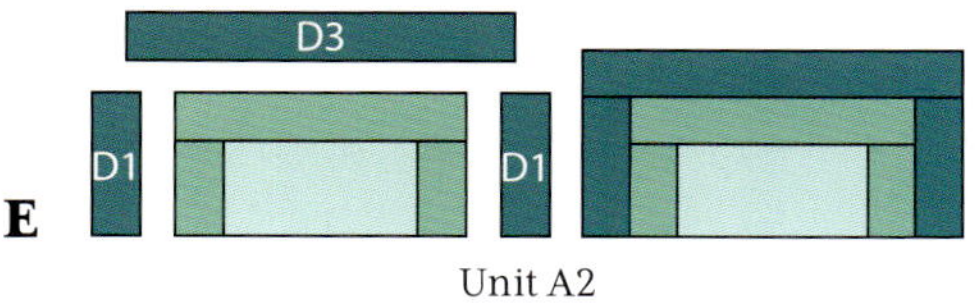

3. Gather 4 H2 rectangles, 8 J1, 4 J3, 8 K1, and 4 K3 rectangles. Arrange them as shown and Repeat Steps 1–2 to make a total of 4 Unit C1s. Unit C1 measures 8½˝ × 16½˝. ***fig. F***

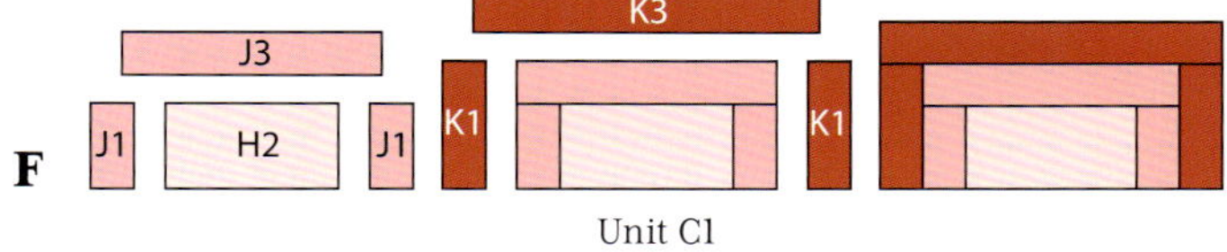

4. Sew 2 J2 rectangles to 2 sides of the H1 square. Press the seams toward the J2 rectangles. Sew 2 J3 rectangles to the top and the bottom of the unit. Press the seams toward J3 rectangles. ***fig. G***

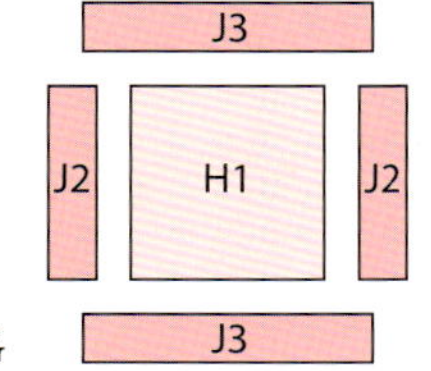

5. Sew 2 K2 rectangles to 2 sides of the Step 4 unit. Press the seams toward K2 rectangles. Sew 2 K3 rectangles to the top and the bottom of the unit. Press the seams toward K3 rectangles. Call this Unit C2, measuring 16½˝ × 16½˝. ***fig. H***

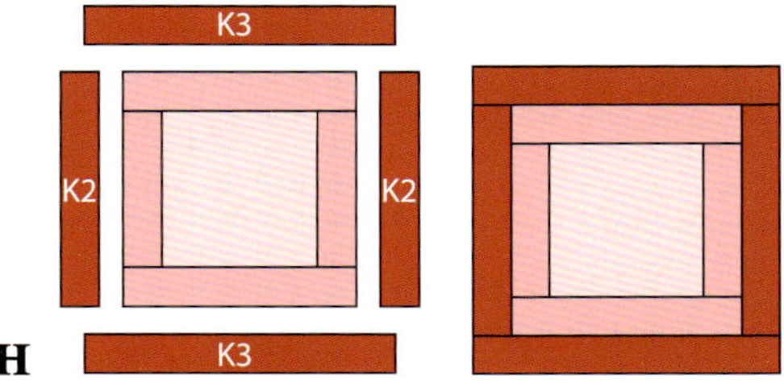

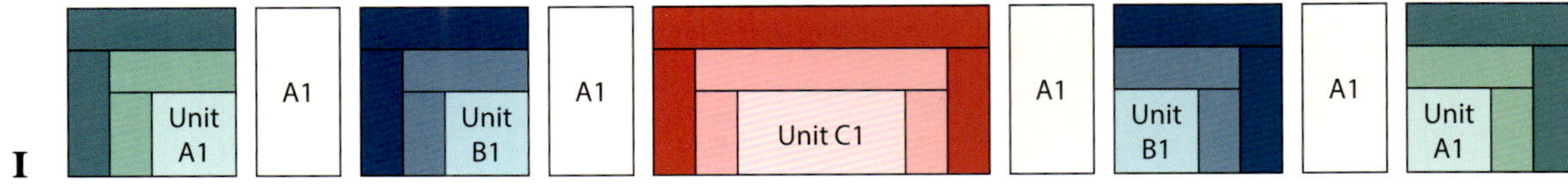

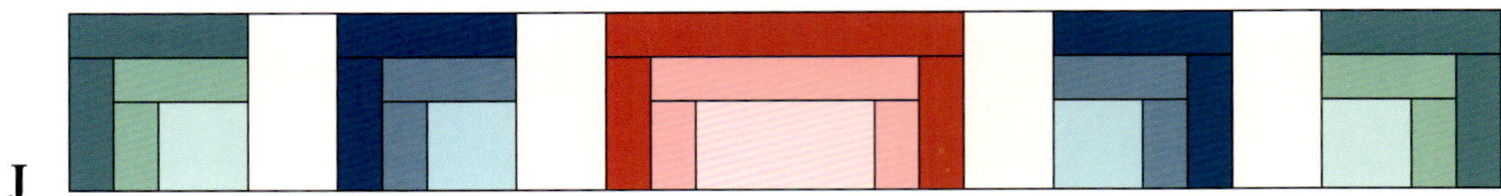

Make Top and Bottom Rows

1. Arrange the following units into a row ***(fig. I)***:

Row: Unit A1, A1 rectangle, Unit B1, A1 rectangle, Unit C1, A1 rectangle, Unit B1, A1 rectangle, Unit A1

2. Sew the units together into a row. Press the seams toward the A1 rectangles. Repeat to make a second unit. Each unit measures 8½″ × 64½″. These are the Top and Bottom Rows. ***fig. J***

Make Column A, B and C

1. Arrange Column A by alternating 4 A1 rectangles with 2 Unit A1s and a Unit A2. Pay close attention to the orientation of each of Unit A1. ***fig. K***

2. Sew the units together and press the seams toward the A1 rectangles. Call this Column A, measuring 8½″ × 48½″. Repeat to make a second Column A. ***fig. L***

3. Arrange the following units (from top to bottom) into a column: Unit B1, A1 rectangle, Unit B1, A2 square, Unit B1, A1 rectangle, Unit B1. Pay close attention to the orientation of each Unit B1. ***fig. M***

4. Sew the units into a column, and press the seams toward the A1 rectangle. Call this Column B, measuring 8½″ × 48½″. Repeat to make a second Column B. ***fig. N***

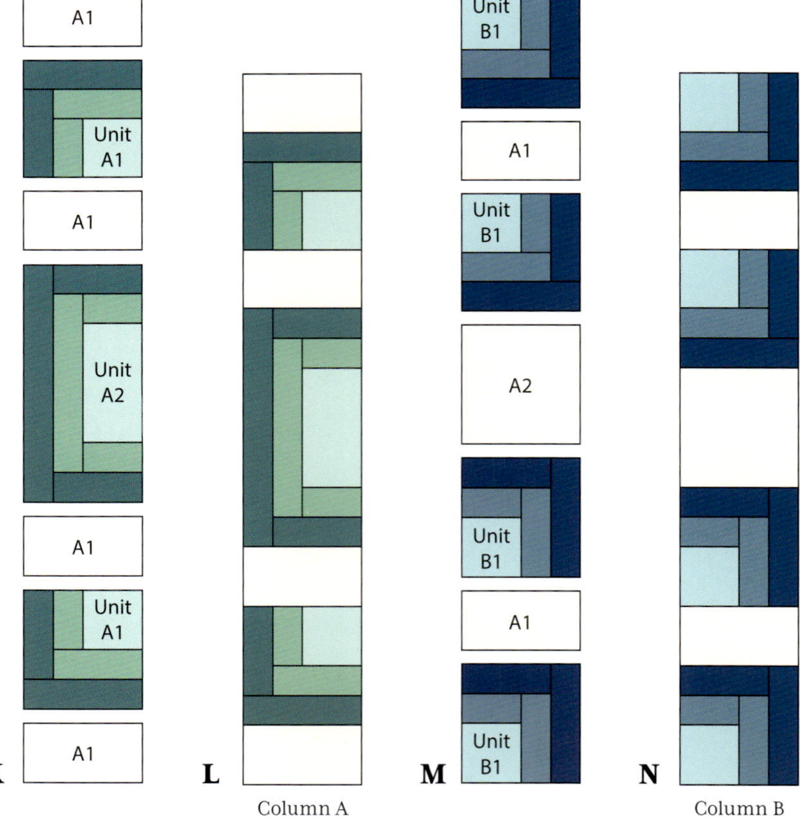

5. Arrange the following units (from top to bottom) into a column: A4 strip, Unit C1, A4 strip, Unit C2, A4 strip, Unit C1, A4 strip. ***fig. O***

6. Sew the units together, and press the seams toward the A4 strips. Call this Column C, measuring 16½″ × 48½″. ***fig. P***

Assemble the Quilt

1. Arrange the columns into the following order (from left to right), paying close attention to the orientation of the columns: Column A, Column B, A3 strip, Column C, A3 strip, Column B, Column A. ***fig. Q***

2. Sew the columns together. Follow the arrows for pressing direction. Call this the Center Unit.

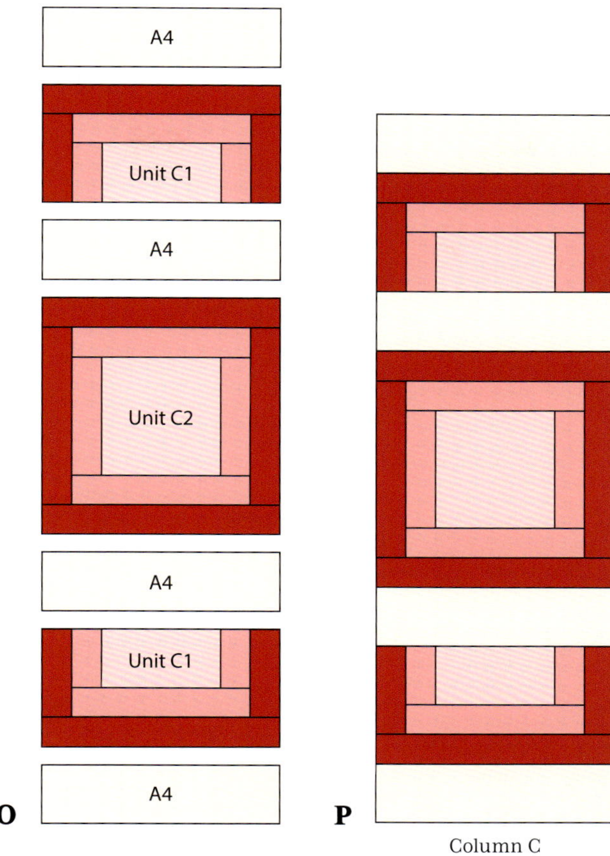

Column C

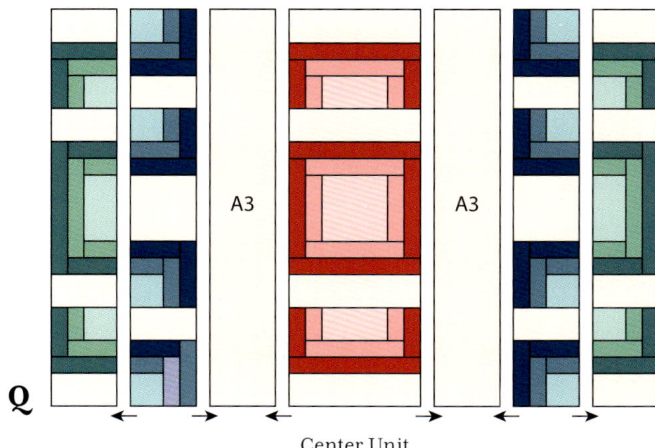

Center Unit

3. Arrange the following units (from top to bottom): A5 strip, Top Row, Center Unit, Bottom Row, A5 strip. ***fig. R***

4. Sew the rows together, and press the seams open or toward the A5 strips.

5. Sew 2 A6 strips to 2 sides of the Step 6 unit. Press the seams toward the A6 strips. The quilt top measures 72½″ × 72½″. ***fig. S***

R

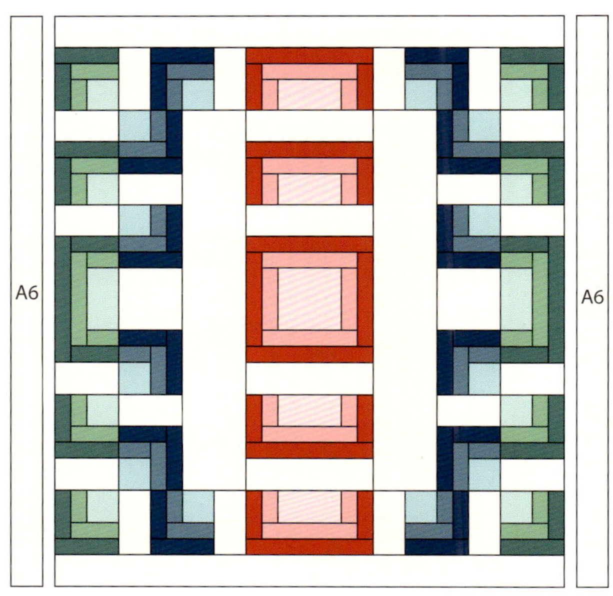

S

Finish the Quilt

Layer, quilt, and bind the project as desired. See Quilt Assembly (page 24).

MINI PROJECT

Golden Meadow Wall Hanging

I hope you're not tired of Log Cabin blocks yet! They're a great way to practice your color-picking skills, and if you prefer, you can turn this project into a pillow or a placemat! For more on sewing Log Cabins, see Cozy Cabin Quilt (page 104).

MATERIALS

Yardages are based on 42″-wide fabric.

Fabric A: ⅓ yard

Fabric B: 1 square 5″ × 5″

Fabric C: 1 square 10″ × 10″

Fabric D: 1 square 10″ × 10″

Fabric E: 1 square 5″ × 5″

Fabric F: 1 square 10″ × 10″

Fabric G: 1 square 10″ × 10″

Fabric H: 1 square 5″ × 5″

Fabric J: 1 square 10″ × 10″

Fabric K: 1 square 10″ × 10″

Binding: ¼ yard

Backing: ⅞ yard

Batting: 29″ × 29″

Fabric

In this quilt, I used Riley Blake Confetti Cotton in Cloud for background fabric and scraps for accent colors.

Finished Project: 21˝ × 21˝
Skill Level: Beginner
Skill Builder: Color Theory

Choosing Quilt Colors

Color is the soul of every quilt. Choosing the right color palette can elevate your quilt from ordinary to extraordinary, creating visual harmony, excitement, or serenity depending on your goals. In this project, we'll dive into three key color schemes—Complementary, Split Complementary, and Triadic—and explore how to apply these to your quilt designs.

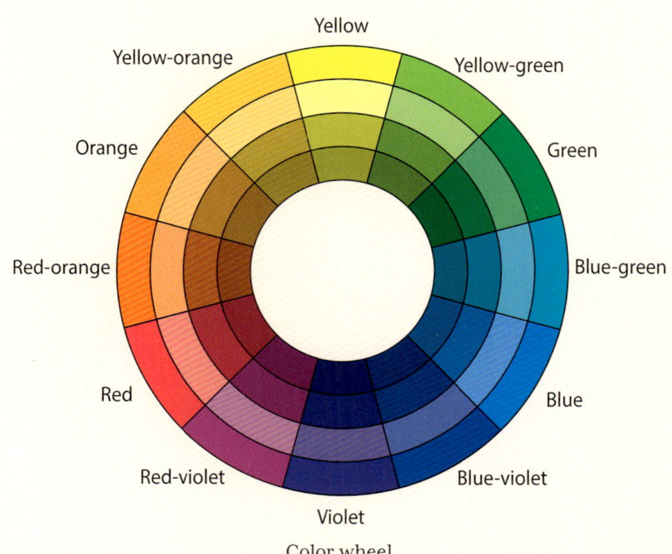

Color wheel

Complementary Colors: Bold and Dramatic

Complementary colors sit opposite each other on the color wheel, which is why they create such bold and vibrant energy. They're perfect for adding strong focal points or striking accents to a quilt. But, use them sparingly. Too much contrast can make your quilt feel a bit overwhelming or chaotic. Balance is key to letting those bold colors shine.

A classic example is red and green colors that are often associated with the festive spirit of Christmas. When used together, they bring a cheerful and lively feel to any quilt, making them perfect for holiday projects.

How it works:

- Red and green are directly opposite each other on the color wheel, making them complementary colors.
- When paired, the warmth of red and the coolness of green enhance each other's brightness, creating a bold and dynamic contrast.
- This combination works because the contrast naturally draws attention and creates a sense of balance between warm and cool tones.

Golden Meadow with direct complementary colors

Split Complementary Colors: Balanced and Versatile

Split complementary color schemes start with one base color, look at its complementary color on the color wheel, then pair it with the two colors *next to* its complementary. This gives you contrast, but in a gentler, more balanced way. It's a great way to add depth and interest to a quilt, without it feeling too busy or overwhelming.

For example, choose orange as the base color to be the main focal point. The split complementary colors for orange are blue-green (teal) and blue-purple (lavender), which are adjacent to blue (orange's complementary color).

How it works:

- Orange provides warmth and energy to the palette.
- Teal offers a cool tone, balancing the warmth of orange and creating harmony.
- Lavender introduces a soft, gentle contrast, adding a delicate touch of coolness that complements the boldness of orange.
- This approach is great for creating visual harmony with just enough contrast to be interesting.

Triadic Colors: Vibrant and Playful

Triadic color schemes use three colors that are evenly spaced around the color wheel. This creates a dynamic and balanced look which is perfect for quilts that feel cheerful and lively. It's a great choice for bold, modern patterns, though it can be a bit tricky to make subtle.

For example, choose blush pink, yellow, and blue to create a harmonious palette.

How it works:

- Blush pink is soft, warm, and gentle. It serves as the focal point, adding a sense of warmth.
- Yellow is a bright and cheerful complement to blush pink. It brings energy and a sense of optimism to the palette, providing contrast to the softer blush.
- Blue is a cool, calming tone, balancing the warmth of blush and yellow, adding depth and sophistication.
- This color combo is perfect for creating a cheerful, balanced, and welcoming vibe, making it ideal for everything from decorating a space to choosing a playful color palette for your wardrobe.

Golden Meadow with split complementary colors

Golden Meadow with triadic colors

CUTTING

The cutting instructions are written for a split complementary color combination, but they can easily be adapted for the complementary and triadic color schemes. Use the labeled diagrams below as your guide to adjust the cutting lists to your preferred version.

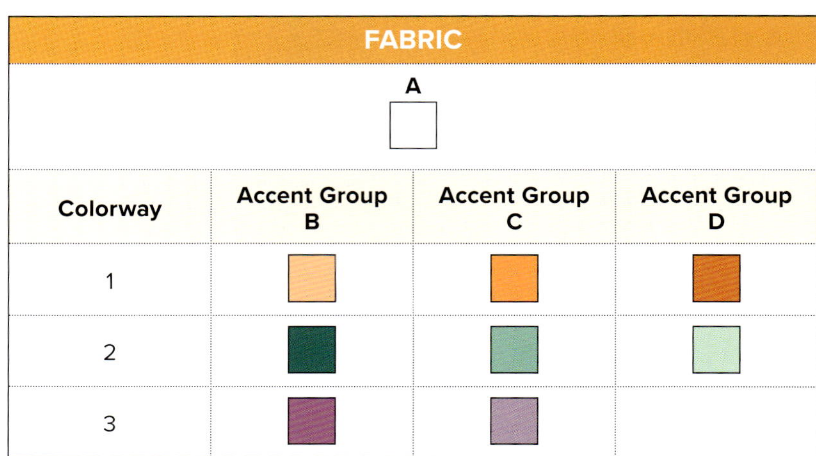

FABRIC			
A			
Colorway	Accent Group B	Accent Group C	Accent Group D
1			
2			
3			

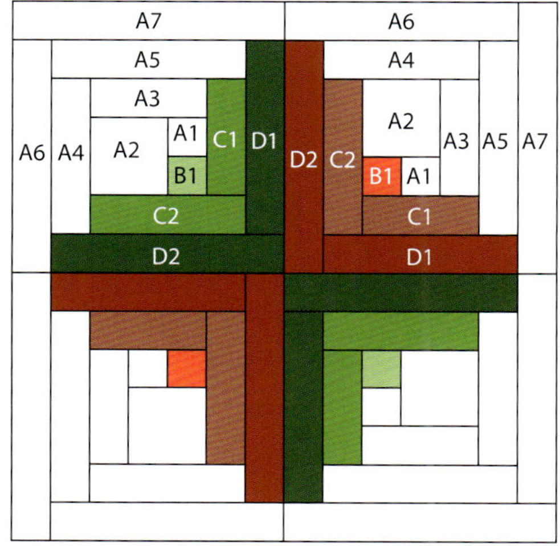

Direct complement

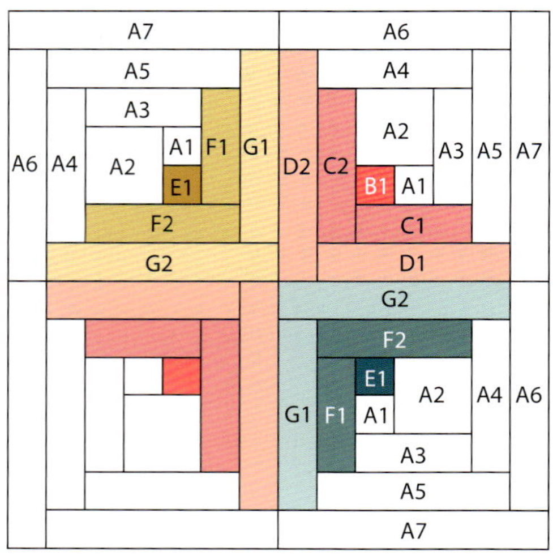

Triadic

Fabric A (Cloud)

Cut 1 strip 4˝ × WOF, subcut into:

- **A2:** 4 squares 3½˝ × 3½˝

Cut the leftover fabric strip 4˝ × 28˝ lengthwise into 2 strips 2˝ × 28˝, then subcut into:

- **A1:** 4 squares 2˝ × 2˝
- **A3:** 4 rectangles 2˝ × 5˝
- **A4:** 4 rectangles 2˝ × 6½˝

Cut 3 strips 2˝ × WOF, sewn and subcut into:

- **A5:** 4 rectangles 2˝ × 8˝
- **A6:** 4 rectangles 2˝ × 9½˝
- **A7:** 4 rectangles 2˝ × 11˝

Fabric B (Light Orange)

B1: 2 squares 2˝ × 2˝

Fabric C (Medium Orange)

C1: 2 rectangles 2˝ × 5˝

C2: 2 rectangles 2˝ × 6½˝

Fabric D (Dark Orange)

D1: 2 rectangles 2˝ × 8˝

D2: 2 rectangles 2˝ × 9½˝

Fabric E (Dark Teal)

E1: 1 square 2˝ × 2˝

Fabric F (Medium Teal)

F1: 1 rectangle 2˝ × 5˝

F2: 1 rectangle 2˝ × 6½˝

Fabric G (Light Teal)

G1: 1 rectangle 2˝ × 8˝

G2: 1 rectangles 2˝ × 9½˝

Fabric H (Dark Purple)

H1: 1 square 2˝ × 2˝

Fabric J (Medium Purple)

J1: 1 rectangle 2˝ × 5˝

J2: 1 rectangle 2˝ × 6½˝

Fabric K (Light Purple)

K1: 1 rectangle 2˝ × 8˝

K2: 1 rectangles 2˝ × 9½˝

Binding

Cut into 3 strips 2¼˝ × width of fabric (WOF).

CONSTRUCTION

Seam allowances are ¼″ unless otherwise noted.

Log Cabin Blocks

1. Arrange the following units around a B1 square as shown. ***fig. A***

2. Sew the units to the starting square, alternating between colors A, C, and D and following the numbers (which indicate the order in which to add the strips). The finished unit (Unit 1) measures 11″ × 11″. Press the seams away from the starting square. ***fig. B***

3. Repeat Steps 1–2 to create a second block.

4. Repeat Steps 1–2 to make the remaining 2 blocks in the other 2 colorways. ***fig. C***

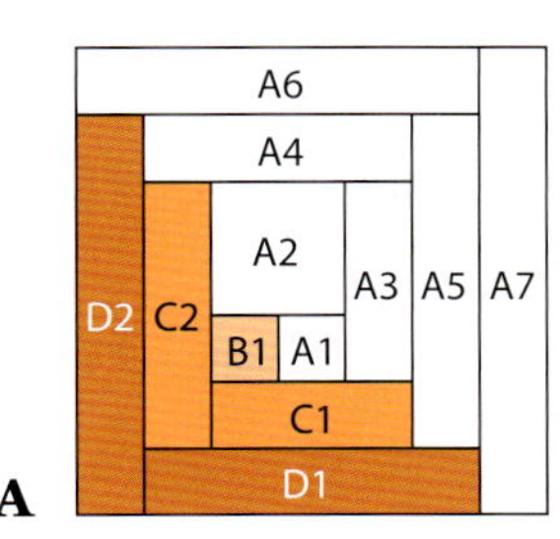

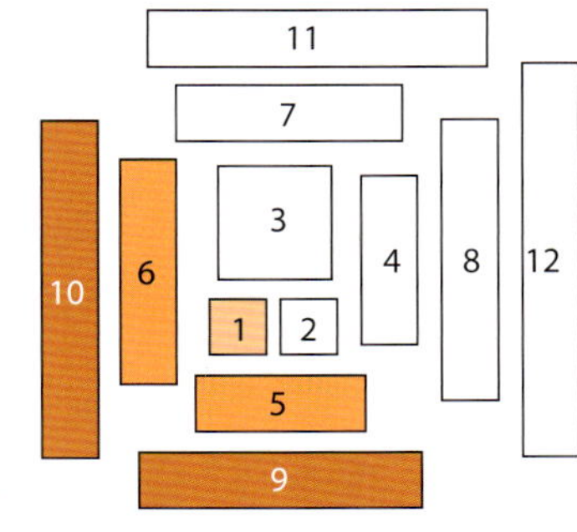

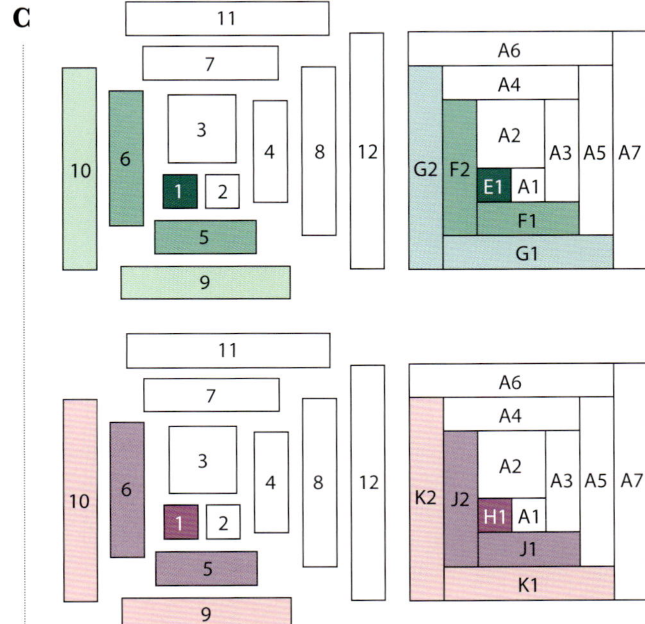

Assemble the Quilt

1. Arrange the units into rows. Pay attention to the orientation of each unit. ***fig. D***

2. Sew the units into rows, then sew the rows together. Press the seams open. The quilt top measures 21½″ × 21½″. ***fig. E***

Finish the Quilt

Layer, quilt, and bind the project as desired. See Quilt Assembly (page 24).

Templates

To access the templates in a PDF download, scan this QR code or go to **tinyurl.com/11638-patterns-download**

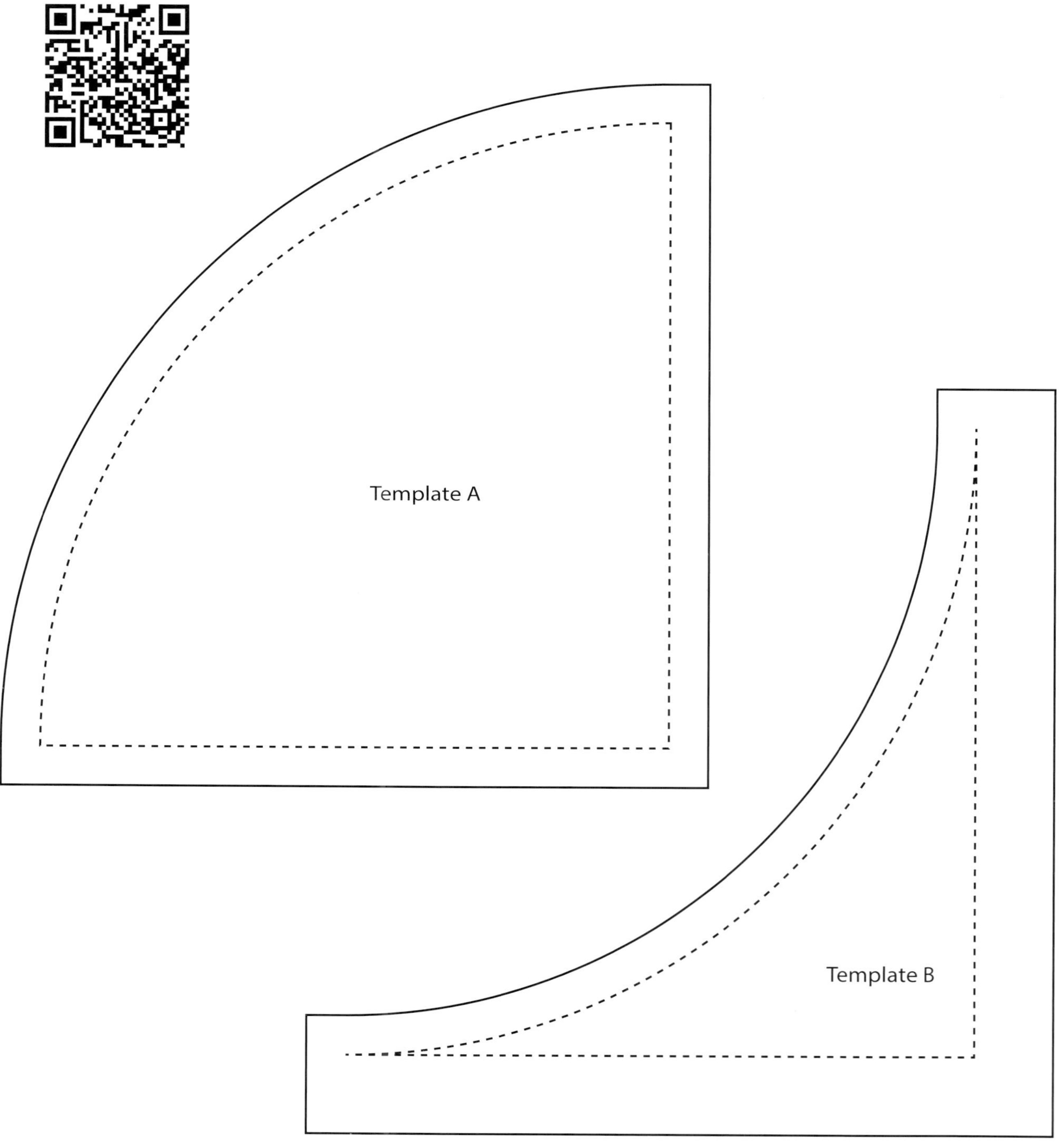

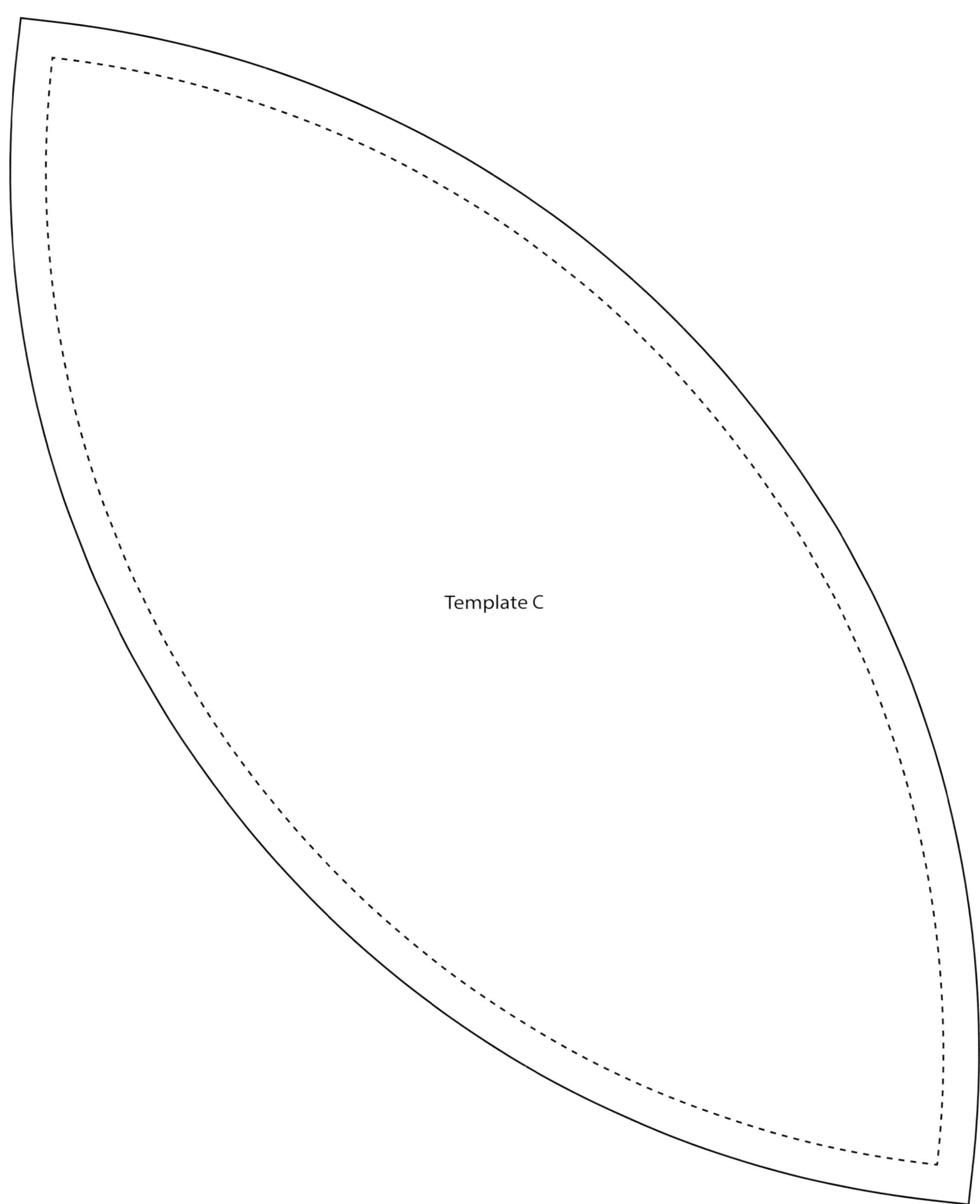
Template C

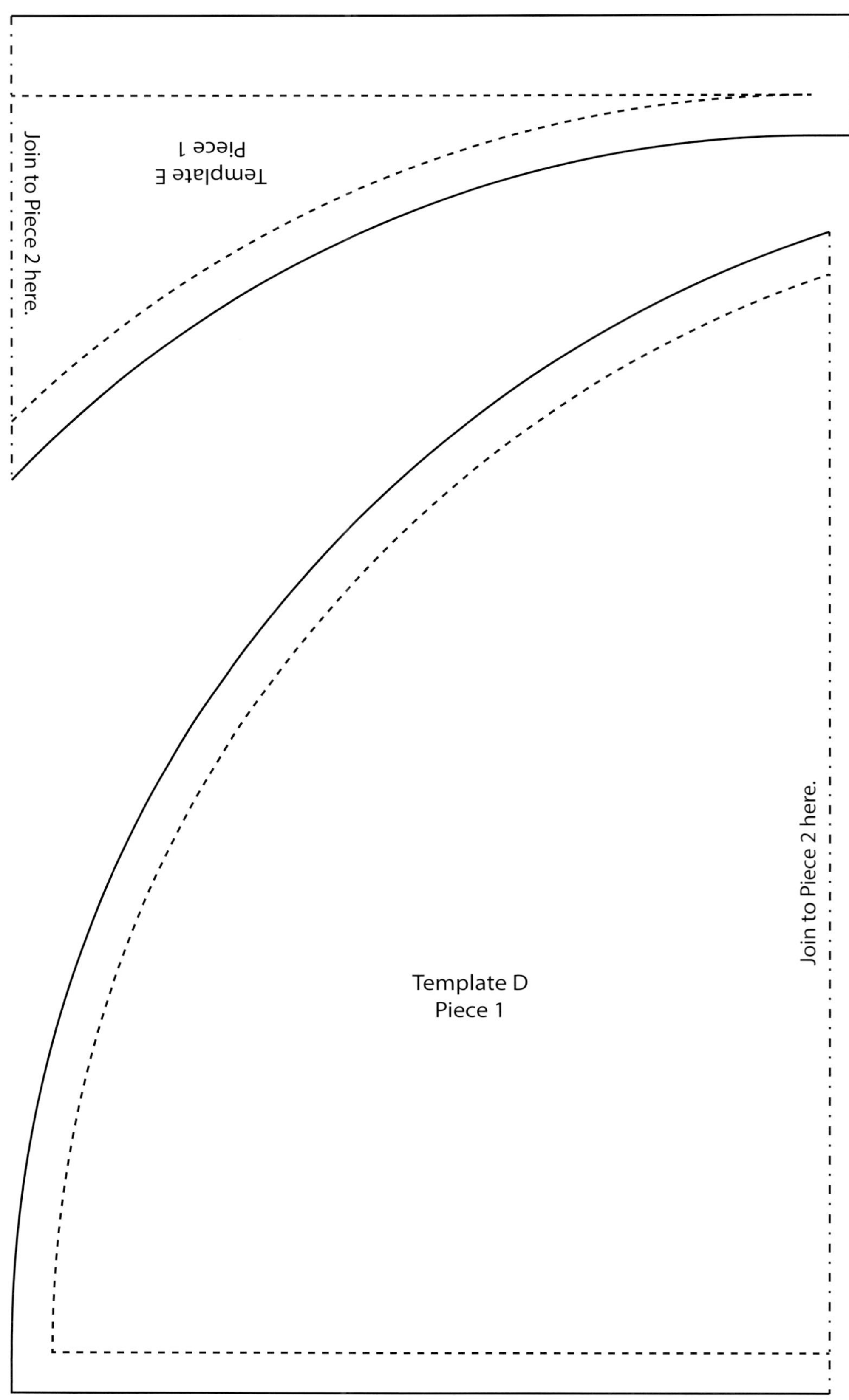
Join to Piece 2 here.
Template E
Piece 1
Template D
Piece 1
Join to Piece 2 here.

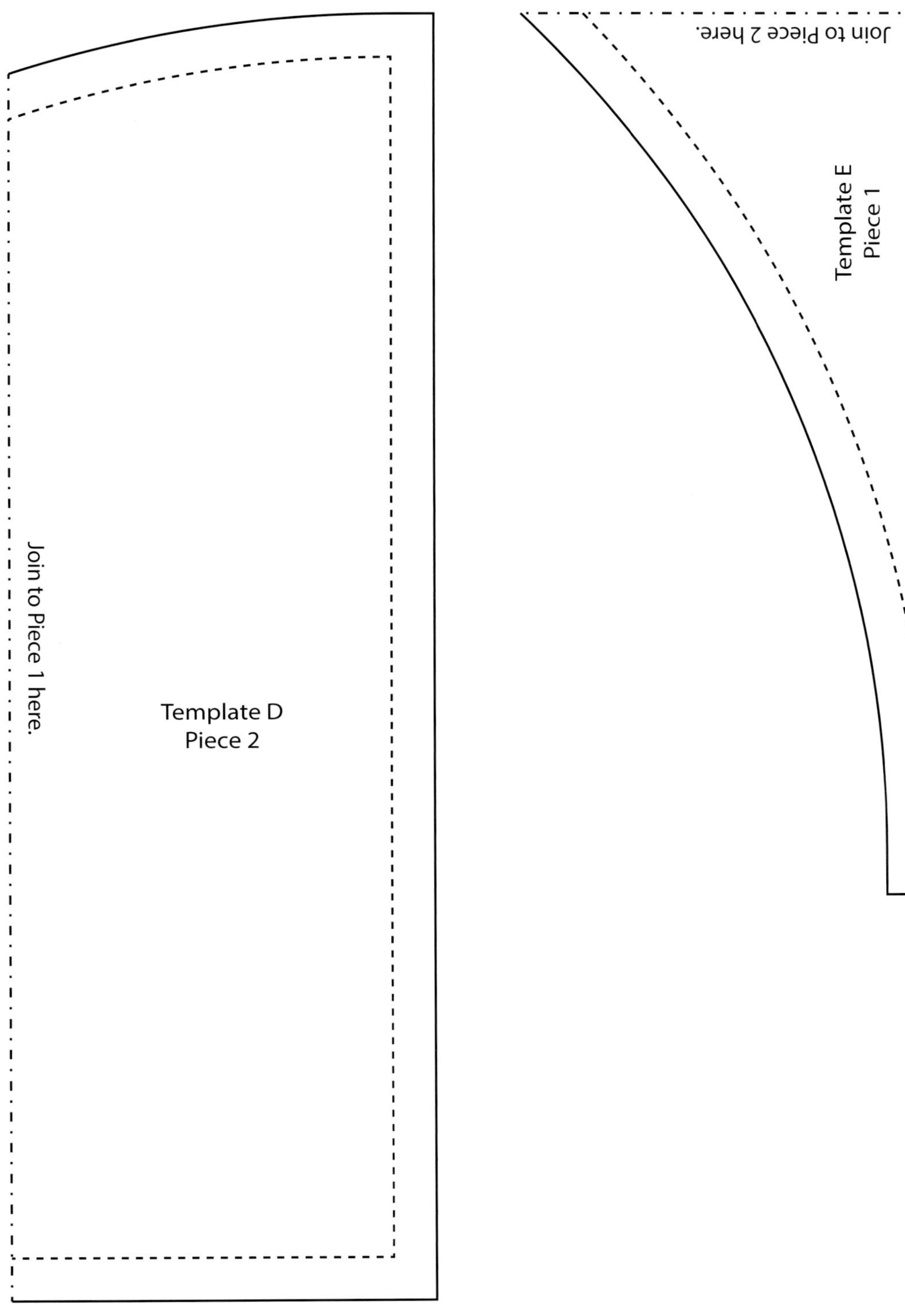
Join to Piece 1 here.
Template D
Piece 2
Join to Piece 2 here.
Template E
Piece 1

About the Author

Sandy Saengsuk, the heart and soul behind Thai Charm, is based in Minnesota. She discovered quilting as a way to create joy and connection through handmade art. Growing up outside Bangkok, she never imagined this craft would become such a meaningful part of her life. Her work reflects a love for vibrant colors and her Thai heritage. She strives to blend traditional quilting with designs that celebrate both creativity and culture. She also runs a longarm quilting business. Find her online **@ThaiCharmllc** and **thaicharmllc.com**

About the Photographer

Lydia Nicholson lives in central North Dakota with her husband and three kids. When she isn't busy with photography or family life, she enjoys reading, baking, and of course, quilting. Find her online **@twopinesphotography** or **twopinesphotography.com**